Ky'

success!
all the best,
Amy

MEDIATION
SUCCESS

GET IT OUT,
GET IT OVER, AND
GET BACK TO BUSINESS!

A Practical Guide to Resolving
Workplace Conflict

AMY L. LIEBERMAN

TABLE OF CONTENTS

INTRODUCTION
WHAT IS MEDIATION?

Mediation is a structured, confidential process where people in conflict seek to resolve their differences with the help of a neutral third party: the mediator or conflict-resolver.

It is not a legal process, in the sense that people who come to mediation are not sworn under oath, do not call witnesses, or introduce exhibits. There is no written decision by a third party. Instead, it is the parties themselves who reach resolution, with the assistance of the mediator or conflict-resolver.

People in litigation frequently seek to mediate their disputes, as a form of "Alternative Dispute Resolution," hoping to resolve the conflict as an alternative to a full-blown trial. In those instances, attorneys are typically involved. Company representatives, often including human resources professionals, also attend. The outcome is a written agreement, which becomes a legally binding resolution. It is generally referred to as a "Settlement Agreement," or a "Settlement Agreement and Release," because it releases all claims against the company.

When people are involved in workplace conflict, as well as partnership or organizational disputes that generate dysfunction within businesses, attorneys are often not involved. Employees seek mediation because their work relationship has become so problematic that they are no longer functioning productively at work. The desired outcome is a written commitment to effect specified behavioral or procedural changes which will improve their relationship in the workplace, and prevent conflict from escalating into a legal claim.

In both of the above circumstances—conflict that is played out in the courtroom or the conference room—the assistance of a third party is needed to help employees and employers resolve tension and conflict that they have been unable to resolve themselves. In both of these instances, the same process of mediation allows everyone involved to get it out, get it over, and get back to business.

Mediation is voluntary, in the truest sense of the word. That's because no solution is imposed on anyone. A mediator is *not* the decision-maker.

It's what the parties believe is fair, or workable, that controls. Instead, the mediator helps each person to explore various aspects of the conflict, to be open to new information, and to consider possible resolutions that may not have been considered before. What the mediator thinks a reasonable resolution *should* be, may or may not have any bearing on the outcome.

The mediator works to reach a resolution that works for all involved. Discussions occur in joint or separate sessions, or both.

When the goal is reached of resolving the conflict in a way that works for all parties, that's Mediation Success. The mediator documents the agreement so that it is a binding settlement, or a commitment to future action in the workplace.

If the parties to the conflict do not agree, there is no resolution, and they can continue with any other avenues of redress available to them, such as proceeding in court, pursuing other formal grievance processes, or perhaps even leaving the company.

Mediation is best facilitated by an experienced, but neutral, third party. That person can be a qualified mediator, or a human resource professional, manager, or supervisor with mediation skills. For legal disputes, there is a greater likelihood of success where the mediator is knowledgeable about the law, especially in the substantive area of the conflict (e.g., employment law, contract disputes, intellectual property, or whatever area of law is at the heart of the dispute).

For both legal matters, and for workplace or executive conflict, the mediator needs to be aware of both interpersonal dynamics and the psychology of conflict. That is where this book comes in.

This book is meant to help all those who are faced with the often daunting task of resolving employee relations issues, organizational conflict, EEOC charges, and lawsuits.

Control Your Destiny with Mediation Success

You can control your destiny and resolve the conflict. You can do this by using mediation, guided by the strategies discussed in this book, to eliminate or reduce the conflict to something that is manageable. Mediation can be an ideal tool to reach an outcome you can live with.

Alleviate the stress, eliminate the drain on resources, and return to productivity. Get it out, get it over, and get back to business.

Why am I so confident you can do this? Because: *mediation works*. Mediation with an experienced mediator is almost always successful. In my experience, well over 90% of the time mediation resolves the conflict, by settling the dispute or improving the relations.

If you had a disease, and your doctor recommended a treatment that was 90% effective, would you take that treatment? Of course you would. If your financial planner recommended an investment with a 90% chance of a positive return, wouldn't you jump at it? Katie bar the door!

In 2011, the EEOC's private sector national mediation program resolved over 9,800 charges—the highest number in the history of the mediation program. The EEOC's goal is to resolve charges within 180 days of filing. In FY 2011, 96.9% of both charging parties (employees) and respondents (employers) reported confidence in the mediation program.

From a business perspective, mediation makes sense as a strategic tool used to eliminate risk. It presents a great return on investment of a small amount of time.

From a personal perspective, mediation makes sense as a venue for resolution that brings personal peace and ultimate healing.

These Mediation Success insights and strategies revealed in this book were developed after more than ten years of practice in working with employment disputes to bring people together, preserve capital resources, and restore productivity.

The Mediation Success approach focuses on the three critical aspects of conflict: the substance of the dispute, the process of obtaining buy-in and agreement, and the psychology of emotion that can prevent resolution.

The Mediation Success strategies will enlighten HR professionals, supervisors, managers, and lawyers helping to resolve serious workplace conflict.

PART ONE:

War and Peace

CHAPTER 1

No One Wins a War at Work

I once had a CEO at one of my presentations ask, "Isn't mediation about winning?"

"No," I told him. "It's about resolution."

Mediation is about reaching an agreement that puts the matter behind you, so you can get it out, get it over, and get back to business.

If people expect to "win," that expectation is not likely to be met. In the book *Conversations with God*, Neale Donald Walsch explains that the greatest source of anger is unmet expectations. If one views conflict as a battle that needs to be won, there is a huge likelihood that the outcome will be more frustration and unhappiness.

Our court system provides a "win-lose" approach to conflict. One side wins, one side loses. Many who are familiar with mediation often call it "win-win." I've heard lawyers call it "lose-lose."

I have a different view of mediation. I call it, "Can live with—can live with."

People generally don't dance out of mediation ecstatically happy, shouting "woo-hoo!" with huge smiles on their faces. Most of the time, they say, "Well, okay, perhaps this is not exactly the outcome I envisioned when I walked in here today. But, all things considered, now that I've had a chance to look at this from a few different perspectives, *this is an outcome I can live with."*

Why do they say that? Because it brings them the peace that comes with resolution.

Mediation Is Not Win-Win:
It's Can Live With-Can Live With

I find that goal to be realistic—and reachable. When I work with people who seek my help to resolve conflict, and we are all together in a conference room to begin a mediation, I explain my "can live with-can live with" view of conflict resolution. I then tell them: "This is my goal for you and for this process today."

Every time I make this statement to roomful of people in conflict, I see smiles of acknowledgement and heads nodding. *Every* time. That's because they realize it is not about winning. It's something they have likely known all along, but have yet to express. They have now opened their mind to the possibility of resolution, in a way different from what they have wanted or insisted upon in the past, by realizing that there may be another outcome they can live with, and get the peace that comes with resolution.

The "Can Live With" outcome is an essential core of the Mediation Success approach to resolving conflict. It brings the peace that comes with resolution.

Mediation Success Rule #1:
Go for the "Can Live With-Can Live With" outcome.

Serious Conflict Exhausts You

If you have ever experienced serious workplace conflict, you know the impact. It's like a battle, and it can leave you "war-weary." The stress is the monster that keeps you up at night, and gives you headaches. Conflict impacts the employee, the organization, and partnerships in unique ways, all of which are negative and hurtful.

Serious Conflict for the Employee

If you are an employee, perhaps you received a warning or other discipline, and you worry you are in danger of losing your job. Or, your boss keeps propositioning you and you are concerned that your lack of response will jeopardize your position. Someone else got that promotion you deserved. You've been treated unfairly, but you are afraid to complain, because you think no one will do anything or your boss will retaliate.

Stress seeps into your home life and causes tension at home. You become irritable and even withdrawn. You consider counseling. You may be on antidepressants or anti-anxiety medication, perhaps for the first time in your life. You feel overwhelmed and powerless.

Wondering about your options, you actually go to a lawyer—gasp! You learn that there is no real legal basis to sue. Or, you learn that you in fact may have a case, but that the process of seeking justice will take years. Not to mention the cost.

You learn that an attorney charges an hourly rate, which you can't afford. Maybe you've found a lawyer who will take your case on a contingent fee (no fees due until the case settles or is resolved through a trial), but you learn you will still be responsible for certain costs of litigation that can run into the thousands of dollars—a price you don't think you can afford.

You feel like you have no options, or at least, no good ones.

Serious Conflict for Organizations

In a small organization, you may have had an EEOC charge filed against you, forcing you to hire counsel. You had no idea it would cost so much just to take the first step of having the lawyer review the information, interview witnesses, and prepare a response to the charge. All that and you aren't even in litigation yet. This is a problem—there was no budget for legal defense.

What about other employees in the organization? If they find out, will they jump on the bandwagon too?

For larger companies, you have been through this before. You know, based on unpleasant past experience, that legal fees can be hundreds of thousands of dollars. You're already into it for, perhaps, $25,000.

You exclaim with frustration: "How could this have happened? We had a policy against this, how can we be liable? When will this end?"

For large and small organizations alike, your key people are spending far too much time dealing with the lawyers, discovery requests, and depositions. Your focus is distracted from important work issues. Business is not getting done like it should.

Serious Conflict for Partners

For the first time, you don't understand why your partner or team member isn't living up to his end of the bargain. All of the sudden you are not seeing "eye to eye." He's not doing the work, not attending meetings, not communicating information.

In larger partnerships, factions have developed. When there's a serious issue, partners are making an "end-run" and engaging in manipulation behind the scenes.

Trust is impaired, effectiveness is reduced, and you're concerned about your long-term ability to succeed as a business. Your partnership agreement doesn't address what to do when there are interpersonal issues, because, frankly, you never anticipated this kind of problem. Now what?

Limitations of the Legal System

The legal system of bringing your case to court—litigation—allows you to seek vindication. But, going to court doesn't always solve the problem.

Winning doesn't always mean you have won, whether you are the employee or the employer. The bitterness of hidden costs, and the psychological or business toll exacted by the litigation process, frequently outweighs the anticipated sweetness of success.

It is vital that anyone involved in the decision to pursue or defend a claim in court be aware of the limitations on our beloved system of justice.

Here's the hard, cold reality.

Mediation Success Rule #2:
Make sure everyone is aware of the limitations of litigation.

1. Litigation is Costly and Destructive

When mediation is held rather early in the process of litigation, a sentiment I frequently hear from plaintiffs (the person bringing the lawsuit) is this: "I am prepared to do whatever it takes. What the company did to me is wrong! I don't care if it takes years."

From the other side of the table, I hear: "We are fighting this! This claim is frivolous! It's a matter of principle!"

Here's a key point: *Principle has an inverse effect on principal.* That means, the longer you insist on standing up for the righteousness of your actions based on "principle," the more your valuable "principal" is depleted.

Your stamina, too, is affected. The court system is not a sprint. It's a marathon.

When mediation is held later in the proceedings, by contrast, this is what I almost always hear: "I just want to move on! I need this to be *done!*" Or: "We just need to stop the bleeding."

These statements come from the fact that the parties did not realize either the immense toll it would take on them to continue the battle emotionally, the amount of focus that would be diverted from their business, or the huge financial cost associated with continued pursuit.

2. "Justice" is a Myth

Serious conflict starts out disrupting your life, and if it's legal in nature, it can land you in court. Yet, the courtroom is the worst place to obtain justice. The justice system allows you to try to persuade a judge or jury that you were right and the other side was wrong. But that's all it does—it allows you to seek vindication, or, in other words, justice. But, it does not guarantee that you will in fact *receive* justice.

According to the *Merriam-Webster Dictionary*, the definition of justice is: "the quality of being just, impartial, or fair." Justice means the trier of fact will hear the whole story, determine the truth, realize that your claim or defense is righteous, and will do the right, reasonable and fair thing: in the case of the plaintiff, award you compensation you believe is fair; or, in the case of the defendant, throwing out the plaintiff's case.

Here's the problem: For justice to prevail, the whole story needs to be told. But, there are limitations on what kind of evidence can come in. This means the whole story may not come out, which in turn, decreases the odds of justice prevailing.

Plus, what also frequently happens is that a witness promises to testify for you, but by the time trial arrives, he moves away or has a change of heart. Even worse, his testimony under oath at trial may not be consistent with what he told you he would say or with what he testified to long ago in deposition. This makes his testimony seem unreliable and unconvincing. Your witness unexpectedly went South, so now, your case is not looking so good.

One case from my early years of practice provides a good example. A female resident in a large apartment complex had left a window open and a man entered her bedroom and sexually assaulted her. The lone security guard on duty that night was wandering the complex and not at his station. When we were preparing the security guard for trial, he explained that the complex was so huge, that there was no way he could have been able to prevent what occurred that night. He felt badly, but it wasn't his fault.

Notwithstanding what he told us before the trial, on the witness stand he broke down in tears, and told the jury, "It's all my fault! If I had been at my station, this may never have happened!" Needless to say, we lost.

The story you know to be true is not always the story that ends up being told. Once again, the chances of "justice" prevailing have decreased.

3. The Outcome is Unpredictable

You never know what will sway the jury. A good lawyer can evaluate the facts of a case in light of the applicable law and ballpark your chances of winning or losing. But, every lawyer who has practiced for any length of time, no matter what side they represent, will tell you stories of when they won cases they should have lost, and lost cases they should have won. It happens all the time.

Even if you *know* you are right, you never know what the jury will relate to, or what they the final outcome will be. They may be swayed by a particular witness, or a certain exhibit, or what a lawyer said. They may disregard what you think is key evidence and go with what *they* think is fair.

Once you get to trial, it's a crapshoot. I once won a case that I tried together with another partner in my firm. We talked to the jury afterwards to find out why they ruled in our favor. We expected to hear it was our stellar cross-examination of the star witness or our spellbinding closing argument.

Unbelievably, they said it was because we "looked so professional." They said, "You both were so coordinated in your dress—the first day, it was navy; the second day, his grey tie matched your suit; the last day, you were crisp in black. You were so much more organized and professional than the other side, we figured you knew what you were doing and were probably right."

I ask you: is that the kind of jury to whom you want to trust your "vindication"?

4. It Takes Years to Get to Trial

It's no secret that getting all the way to trial takes a long time—at least a year, more likely two. A breach of contract or other claim filed in a state court might get to trial within a year or so; a federal court claim often takes longer.

For a claim of employment harassment or discrimination, you would typically file in federal court. In order for you to have a "right to sue" in federal court, you must first file an administrative charge with the EEOC.

There are time limitations in which a charge must be filed. You cannot go to court until the EEOC processes your claim. If they investigate it (they don't always do so, as they are very busy) it can take over a year.

Before the EEOC will give you a "right to sue" letter, they will either give you a letter that says they found "no cause" to believe discrimination occurred, or they will give you a "cause" finding, which is a letter stating they have found "reasonable cause" to believe that discrimination occurred.

This is not the end of the road. The "cause" finding does not mean you win. All it does is give you the "right to sue" in court.

In many jurisdictions, the EEOC's finding will be admissible in court. The employer, though, has the right to argue in court that the "cause finding" was in error, because the EEOC investigator did not have all the relevant information, did not interview key witnesses, or was somehow biased.

Confronted with a "cause finding," an employer might be more likely to settle, but there is no guarantee.

Once you have that piece of paper giving you a right to sue, whether cause is found or not, you have 90 days under federal law to bring suit in federal court. State law claims may have a different time limit.

Filing an EEOC charge costs nothing. There are no fees to do this. However, to bring a lawsuit in court, although you could file "pro per" (without a lawyer), you really need a lawyer at this point if you truly want a good shot at succeeding. Not fun.

You could always ask the EEOC to skip the investigation, and just give you the "right to sue" letter. They will do so. However, you lose the benefit of a no-cost investigation that might provide some validation of your claim. And, again, you go right to the lawyer.

Don't get me wrong. I love lawyers—I am one! I just know it's stressful and costly to go down that road.

5. A Huge Victory is Not Always Best

Here's a scary thought: for the plaintiff employee, a tremendous "win" may not be the best ultimate outcome. This is because a losing employer is not likely to whip out the checkbook and write that check for a million dollars.

The huge victory only increases the likelihood of an appeal. This draws out the process even longer, because the appeal process takes years.

The victory does put you in a better position to negotiate a larger settlement, but it does not mean you will receive every penny of the "win."

6. Winning Costs Money Too!

I once tried an employment case on behalf of an employer, and won. The employee, who had been seeking about $100,000, appealed the decision, and this time, he won. The case was sent back for retrial. The employee won, and this time, the employer appealed, and won.

The case was finally over. Length of time for the whole process? 8 years. Cost to the employer to defend a $100,000 claim? Over half a million dollars. That, my friends, is one hollow victory.

So, you now know some significant limitations. There is no guarantee of justice, it takes a long time to actually get through the court process, it is immensely stressful and it can be hugely expensive.

There is one more important limitation to our legal system.

7. The Court Process Doesn't Apply to Interpersonal Conflict

Your dispute may not be legal in nature. You might be working in a "hostile work environment" that's not, technically by legal definition, "hostile."

Many people don't realize that to have a right to sue legally for a "hostile work environment" the conduct needs to be "hostile" in violation of a specific law that gives you some protection.

"Hostile work environment" is a term of art under Title VII of the Civil Rights Act of 1963, as amended. In other words, hostility alone isn't enough. Your employer must be hostile to you in violation of a protected reason—for example, because of your gender, because you are over 40 years of age, because you are a certain religion or ethnic or national origin, or because you have a disability.

If your manager is simply "hostile" to you because he doesn't like you, or because he plays golf with the other guy, he may just be treating you unfairly, but not illegally.

Another example is where an employer makes a mistake in its conclusion that an employee engaged in wrongdoing, and fires the employee. The employer has a good faith belief that the employee engaged in wrongdoing—but the employee knows the conclusion is wrong. This is unfair, but not necessarily illegal.

Yet a third situation of "unfair but not illegal" may be where a customer complains about an employee. The employer takes the view that the customer is always right, so you are disciplined, or worse, fired. This might seem unfair, but, if the employer takes this position with all employees as a matter of policy or practice, it's likely not illegal.

In short, "unfair" is not the same as "illegal." The court system of justice provides no relief to things that are merely unfair.

Finally, you might be in a partnership or other business relationship that is falling apart based on lack of communication.

Where interpersonal issues are the real reason, the court system is not the right place to seek relief.

Closing Thoughts

1. Conflict is adversarial and takes a huge toll.
2. Principle has an inverse relationship to principal.
3. Expecting to win can lead to frustration and disappointment.
4. The legal system has many significant limitations.
5. The "Can Live With" outcome is realistic and brings peace.

CHAPTER 2

Get to Peace: Mediation Success

To understand why mediation success is the answer to serious conflict in the courtroom or the conference room, it's important to understand a bit about the nature of conflict.

What causes conflict? Why is it so stressful? Why can't we just get past it?

The Causes of Conflict

Conflict can be defined as "friction or opposition, resulting from actual or perceived differences or incompatibility." Another source defines it as "a fight, battle, or struggle, especially a prolonged struggle, strife." Conflict causes us to feel tension and pressure, because we believe someone—or a group of people—is standing in our way, and causing us harm. They are preventing us from achieving our goals, or meeting our needs. This, we believe, is unfair.

Most of us hate conflict. Our reaction to conflict is negative—fight or flight!

Most of us tend to perceive conflict as "bad." It's easy to tell why we feel that way. Conflict creates tension and stress. It produces anxiety. That tension and stress produces deep emotions of fear, anger, resentment, and frustration.

These emotional reactions, in turn, lead to physical symptoms or manifestations, such as an upset stomach, tension headaches, or a tight feeling in our chest. We lose sleep, which affects our health and well-being. Our appetites change. We overeat, or fail to eat at all. We can end up with extreme weight gain or loss.

We withdraw from relationships, or become confrontational.

A friend of mine who is a business consultant always says, "I *hate* conflict!" Whenever she was challenged on payment terms, she caved in, immediately. It took years before she was able to negotiate good business deals for herself. She needed a "coach" to support her in asserting her value.

Tough conflict often generates that "fight or flight" response. When it came to "fight or flight," my consultant friend flew.

When we are tense, we become angry, resentful, worried or fearful.

At work, when we believe we have been treated unfairly or that we are not respected, our behavior changes. We may not focus as well on our projects. We become irritable, which affects our interactions with others. We raise our voices and become accusatory. We "fight" and sometimes, we say things we don't mean, just because we are so angry.

Most of us hate conflict. Our reaction to conflict is negative—fight or flight!

Other bad things happen. We miss deadlines. We skip a meeting. Or two. If we are not well-rested because we are tossing and turning at night, we are not able to perform as well. We take sick leave. I have seen situations where an employee with a serious conflict at work uses up months of leave for stress-related reasons.

In extreme situations, we *literally* stop working—we quit. That is a true "flight" response. This presents an even greater problem if we need our jobs.

Working with the process of mediation, though, you can be supported in seeing conflict another way. As you will later see, it's possible to view facts and circumstances underlying the conflict in another light: one that offers opportunity, instead of danger.

Mediation Success Rule #3:
Focus on the positive outcomes and opportunities that can come from conflict.

Why Does Mediation Work?

To understand how and why mediation success happens, let's start with a few fundamental truths about how we often handle ourselves in conflict.

Sometimes we can be our own worst enemies. We say something we don't mean. As soon as we've said it, we know it was the wrong thing to say. Yet, we do nothing to "take it back."

We take a position we know is adversarial, and we stick to it. We know the other side won't agree, yet, we don't budge. We believe we are reasonable, so, even though it gets us nowhere, we continue to hold firm. We aren't moving—or at least, not until the other side moves. But they haven't moved, so we're stuck. In short, we are stubborn. Once we are locked in, we stop asking. We stop hearing. We can get so caught up in our own anger and righteousness that there is no room in our minds, or for that matter, in our hearts, for change.

We want to resolve things, to get to a better place, but we don't know how. We've been acting a certain way for so long, or the other people have, that our behaviors have become "habits."

We have given up hope. It appears things will never change. All indicators lead us to believe we have hit a dead end, and we have no energy left within us to try anymore. We have no hope. Why bother trying?

We are deeply invested financially and psychologically in a particular position. As a result, we feel we must stay the course. Otherwise, that "investment" is wasted.

We no longer see opportunity. There may be a way to bridge the gap, but we can no longer see it. We don't know what we don't know. These fundamental truths about how we handle conflict present roadblocks, which in turn become obstacles to progress, preventing resolution.

We are not perceived as objective by the other side, and so our views are discounted. Even if our positions or solutions might be reasonable, they are rejected simply because they came from an interested party who seems motivated only to help themselves.

Mediation Conquers the Obstacles

Quite simply, mediation works because it conquers the obstacles.

It provides a forum for respectful communication, and a process to stop people for making harmful statements they can't take back.

It creates an environment where the parties are able to hear, receive, and absorb new information, whether from those with whom they are in conflict or from an objective third party. It provides the dignity of a new rationale, which allows people to consider changing the way they view the situation, and alter their position.

Mediation reveals opportunity. It instills hope. It opens the door to resolution, so people can get it out, get it over and get back to business.

Mediation success in court cases means a settlement agreement.

Mediation success in organizations means a change in how the parties feel about the conflict, and about each other, so that they commit to acting differently in terms of how they treat each other. Mediation success means people follow through with that commitment.

Changed behavior, ultimately, leads to a better, healthier way of dealing with one another. So, mediation brings the peace that comes from the absence of tension.

Let's take a look at three examples of how mediation success worked to open the door, resolve the conflict and move on, in non-legal scenarios—between individuals, in a larger work group, and in a partnership.

Serious Individual Conflict: David and George

David, who had been with the company for 15 years, loved his job as a manager. George was a brand new Executive Vice President and had only come on board nine months earlier. George was David's new boss.

David felt that George did not appreciate his value and his experience. He tried to have informal conversations with George to establish a rapport, but to no avail. George just didn't seem to have the time. He seemed quite formal and standoffish.

David, tired of being rebuffed and minimalized, complained to Human Resources as well as to all the employees that he worked with and supervised. A small mutiny formed. Suddenly, the team refused to complete their tasks on time. A formal "hostile work environment" complaint was made to Human Resources.

HR had a lawyer investigate, but the lawyer found there was no legal basis for a "hostile work environment" complaint under Title VII. Yet, tensions persisted. Human Resources suggested mediation.

Three mediation sessions were held. In the first session, David complained that George seemed not to realize the extent of the David's knowledge and experience. David told George that he did not feel respected or appreciated, and it was important for him to have a rapport with his boss. He wanted to feel valued and liked. David felt his efforts to connect were ignored, and that George spent no time communicating his needs and expectations to David.

George, on the other hand, told David that he had a lot of tasks to accomplish in the huge organization. He worked late most every night. Building a "rapport" was not high on his list. He simply wanted to get his work done in the most efficient way possible. "Schmoozing" was not on his priority list, or any other list, for that matter. He was willing to meet with David, but not whenever David stopped by to chat. It was too distracting and interrupted George's ability to focus on projects. George preferred e-mail to in-person impromptu meetings.

It was clear that George believed that David's complaints were much ado about nothing.

In our mediation, we discussed that it is not unusual for people to want to feel a connection with those whom they work for. George came to realize that rapport was extremely important, not only to David but to other staff as well. He began to see that most people wish to feel fulfilled at their job and will feel more fulfilled when they experience at least some connection to those they work with all day.

Put simply, we want to be liked. When that connection is non-existent, it will lead to complaints—and, legal or not, complaints require attention.

Both men realized that to get past the barrier of resentment that had been established, it would be important for each to bend to accommodate each other's needs. They recognized a blend of both in-person and e-mail communications were necessary. David agreed to develop a formal "Weekly Activities" report. George agreed to meet weekly for an hour on Fridays to review the report and informally discuss any other issues David wished to discuss.

Even better, George began adding at least ten minutes a day to his "task list" to connect with his staff for no critical business reason—just to walk around, say hello, ask how their week has gone, and to focus time each day to building rapport with his staff.

George realized that time spent "connecting" was not a waste of time, but served an important business purpose: employees who feel valued, liked, and respected are less likely to bring claims or to cause dissension.

By the second mediation session, a few weeks later, David and George both reported improved communication and satisfaction with their work relationship.

Several months later, I followed up with both men via e-mail to see how things were going. Both David and George reported that mediation helped them get to a much better place in their working relationship, which in turn improved the morale of the entire team. The initial tensions were gone, and they were able to work effectively together. Mediation success.

Serious Organizational Conflict: Sam and His Work Group

A similar situation occurred in a group of nine people, who worked for a government agency. One of the group, Sam, had complained to their leader about what he believed to be inappropriate and unethical behavior, related to their use of city vehicles. The vehicle issue was investigated, with the conclusion that nothing illegal, unethical, or otherwise inappropriate occurred.

The employee had every right to raise a concern, and the agency did the right thing, in turn, by investigating. Yet, a few of the employees who were investigated were angry that they would be accused of anything improper. They were deeply resentful. They talked to others and the office became divided. Tensions escalated, and the group's ability to function effectively as a team was negatively impacted.

As a group they had begun to interpret every action Sam took as motivated by a desire to make himself look good while making them look bad. Complaining about him to their boss became a daily activity. It impacted productivity; their boss threw his hands up and knew something had to be done to diffuse the situation.

The agency sought my assistance in working with the group, to see if the working relationship could be improved. In mediation with the group, what ultimately came out bore no resemblance to what everyone thought was the cause for the tension, the fact that he filed a complaint.

Here was the heart of the matter: the group thought that the employee believed he was "better than them." They thought this because, each morning when he came in to the office, he did not say "hello." He did not greet his fellow co-workers but went straight to his desk to begin working. When he left, he did not say "goodbye." He ate his lunch on his own. And, he installed a mirror on his cubicle so that he could see what others were doing nearby. They expressed that he did not do anything to be "part of the team."

Sam acknowledged the truth of their statements. He saw no need to say hello or goodbye. He was "only there to work." Yet, he had worked with these people for over ten years. None of them ever felt a connection with him.

Sam believed it was entirely inappropriate for his coworkers to raise this issue. He did not want to have to be "friends" with them.

I encouraged the group to tell him why it was that his self-imposed isolation bothered them, to explain how it impacted them. One of them explained that it made them not want to work with him, to consult with him on projects, or to share key information.

After the mediation session, Sam took some time to absorb the comments. Although he was not motivated by the same need to be liked, he was motivated by financial security: he did not want to lose his job, and he realized he needed the cooperation of the group to perform his job well.

Sam began to change his ways, and at least give a simple "good morning" to his co-workers. One step at a time, the working relationship improved, and the team returned to productivity. Mediation Success.

Serious Partnership Conflict: Cory and Suzanne

For Cory and Suzanne, business partners in a marketing firm, work/life balance seemed to be the biggest issue. Business was booming: they had more business than they could handle. The problem was that in recent months, their relationship had deteriorated. They had several blow-ups, and stopped speaking to one another. They didn't really know why it was happening.

Their communication had broken down. Weekly meetings to discuss projects and strategy had turned into monthly meetings. They were not able to effectively anticipate problems. Deadlines were met—but with only hours to spare. Tensions built, frustrations grew, and the problems seemed insurmountable.

The women considered themselves friends as well as partners, and the tension impacted both their professional and personal lives. Both women realized their business was at serious risk.

In mediation, Cory eventually felt safe enough to confess what was really bothering her: she resented the amount of vacation time Suzanne took, and the timing of her vacations. Suzanne always seemed to take time off on short notice, just before Cory herself would need to be out of town for a business-related reason. Cory was overworked, and felt unfairly disadvantaged.

Suzanne expressed that she felt that Cory was too detail-oriented and tended to "micro-manage." She got her work done on time, and did not want to have to report her every step. For personal reasons, Suzanne needed to regain some balance in her life. Time off was critical to her. Suzanne felt pressure from Cory and reacted by shutting down and withdrawing.

Their partnership agreement said nothing about time off. For Suzanne, balance between work and home was a central focus of her life. The business was really Cory's brain-child, so Cory's focus was on growth of a vital business.

Here, mediation led to a different outcome than the first two situations. Both partners were able, in a safe environment, to share thoughts they had not been able to do before.

Ultimately, they both separately came to the same conclusion: they realized that trying to force a round peg into a square hole was not going to work, and parting ways on a positive note was a better option than staying together. It was a tough decision, but one they both felt good with, as they spent the time working to understand the core issues.

Mediation Success happened another way: They parted knowing they had opened up, learned what was important, and made the right choice. They parted with no regrets.

Closing Thoughts

1. Conflict results from our perception that someone is standing in the way of our success.
2. Conflict generally leads to a fight or flight reaction.
3. We tend to act in ways that create obstacles to resolution.
4. Mediation works because it overcomes those obstacles.
5. Mediation works because it creates a respectful environment where people are able to hear, receive and absorb new information.
6. Mediation works because it provides the dignity needed for others to consider changing their views and alter their position, allowing them to move on personally and professionally!

CHAPTER 3

Get There: The Mediation Success Process

What is Mediation Success?

Mediation Success is not about winning; it's about *resolving*. It's about solving a conflict, or settling a matter, so people can move on.

Get it out, get it over, and get back to the business of both productive work, and the business of enjoying life.

With a legal dispute that's asserted in court, an EEOC charge, or a letter setting forth a legal demand, Mediation Success is a settlement agreement, where the case is resolved and dismissed. The parties move on.

Mediation Success can also be improved relations at work. In the workplace, Mediation Success is about sharing perspectives, gaining greater understanding of what is important to everyone involved, and making future-focused decisions that feel right.

Reasons for frustration or resentment are shared. Respectful communication occurs. Understanding develops. Acknowledgements or commitments are made. People feel better, relationships are improved, and they return to productivity at work. That's success.

Mediation Success is also greater understanding about whether to stay or whether to go. In partnerships and organizations, Mediation Success can also mean that people have come together, fully explored the cause of their differences, and mutually realize it's best to part ways. To accomplish that parting with dignity and respect is Mediation Success. Where each party feels confident they have done all they could to repair the relationship, instead of a deep wound that does not heal, they can feel good about their decision to part and become better able to move on with their lives.

Overview of the Mediation Success Process

Mediation is not the same as conversation. We have conversations every day.

Mediation is goal-directed. Mediation calls for facilitated dialogue, with a structured process. It is a delicate dance of discussion, held solely for the purpose of resolving conflict.

Mediation Success is not about winning; it's about resolving.

Mediation typically takes anywhere from a few hours, to a full day. On occasion, sessions might occur on separate days.

For all types, the Mediation Success process is the same.

The Mediation Success Process

The Mediation Success Process has four steps:
1. Get it Going
2. Get it Out
3. Get it Over
4. Resolve the Conflict

This approach has been developed based on over ten years of resolving workplace conflict and employment disputes. In this chapter, you will have a quick overview of the process and you will develop an understanding of why it works.

Later chapters will give specific information on these steps, with examples, so you can have all the knowledge you need to resolve conflict.

24

Step 1 – Get It Going: Set the Stage for Success

Select Your Mediator. First, decide who should serve as the conflict-resolver. It can be an external qualified employment mediator or it can be an internal mediator, such as a human resource professional or other manager with experience and training in resolving conflict. Look for someone with solid communication skills, who is viewed as a neutral person, and who is dedicated, patient and persistent. Ideally, the person should have a strong intuitive sense and knowledge of key emotional and psychological factors that influence conflict.

Hold the Initial Joint Session. The very first thing a mediator should do is warmly welcome everyone to the mediation. He or she sits at the head of the conference table, with the parties, and their representatives, if any, on either side.

Here, when everyone is together in a joint session, is where the most important work occurs. It is up to the mediator to set the stage for success.

Introductions are made, and ground rules of communication are established and agreed to. The mediator explains the agenda for the session and reinforces the goal of reaching resolution. Information is shared about how and why resolution is likely to occur.

This first part of the process is all about the mediator outlining and taking control of the process. The mediator or conflict-resolver must provide critical reassurance to the people in the room. The fact is that, at this point, the parties have not been able to get to resolution themselves. They need to trust that the person working as their mediator has the skill and ability to keep the process in hand, so they will get to the end goal of peace.

Get it Going means setting the stage for success. If this is done correctly, the mediation has a better chance of going smoothly, as the mediator or manager will have all the tools needed to address and resolve the conflict. Setting the stage will include establishing rapport with the parties, building trust, obtaining agreement on ground rules, and revising expectations so that those expectations are both optimistic and realistic.

In some cases, a joint session is not advisable, which may be determined by the mediator after consultation with the parties or counsel. In that case, the items noted above would simply be discussed individually with each side.

To "get it going" properly, the use of specific words and phrases is essential to help open the minds of the parties and to create a safe environment. You will see how the technique of "selective language" is such a valuable conflict management tool, and learn how to set the stage for success quickly and effectively.

Step 2—Get It Out: Reach the Real Issue

Invite Sharing. During the joint session, the mediator invites each person to share his perspective about what brought them to this point. It is important for the real underlying concerns and interests to be revealed, so they can be addressed.

It is not unusual for all the interests and true driving forces of desires to be unknown until the actual mediation itself, because sometimes we simply do not realize how important something is until we really dig deep.

Full and total discovery and revelation of the real issue, the real driving force, often occurs later, when the mediator meets with the people privately, in separate session. That is because often, people are reluctant to "spill all" in front of the other side.

After the initial joint session, the mediator separates the sides into separate rooms, and engages in shuttle diplomacy, meeting sequentially with each group.

Getting it Out is important. But what is the "it" that needs to be shared? The mediator, manager, or human resource professional needs to recognize the root cause of the conflict. What is the driving force that has been compelling the person to escalate conflict?

Often, people think they know what is truly motivating them to take a certain position, but in the process of mediation they say something which reveals that the real interests are deeper and previously unrealized. The same is true for the driving forces that compel the other side to take their position.

When a person hears herself speak, as she struggles to explain, she gains clarification simply from the process of verbalizing her thoughts. She answers a question or two, and in providing the explanation, gains greater understanding of what is really driving her. She might actually have been unsure of what the true issue was, or the main problem that has been causing so much angst. Only after candid talk does she fully grasp the root cause of the conflict.

For the speaker, it is important to be fully heard, so that the full benefit of "getting it out" is realized for her.

There is equal benefit for the listener. One of the most important aspects of mediation is that it allows new information to be shared.

The reason "getting it out" is so important is that we take positions based on what is known. When new information is shared, new knowledge is gained, and it causes us to re-evaluate our positions.

Perhaps a change in position is warranted, based on learning something we did not know before. Maybe there was nothing new factually that we learned, but the degree of passion, or the key focus, is not what we thought.

Step 3—Get It Over: Embrace the Emotion

Accept the Emotions. Whether in joint session, or in separate meetings, anger, frustration, resentment, and irritation can be expressed. Adrenaline gets going, and the resultant expression of emotion can be overwhelming. There can be tears (in fact, there almost always are), arm waving, yelling, pacing, table-pounding, use of profanity, and even the exclamation, "I'm out of here!"

Accepting and even embracing strong emotion is an essential skill of the mediator. The goal is not to talk about the issues without emotion. The goal is to work with the emotion, so that it will not serve as a block to resolution.

As mentioned above, it is essential to allow each other to be *fully heard.* In addition to the need to learn substantively what the root cause or underlying interest is that is compelling the conflict to escalate, it is equally important to realize the emotional healing that occurs when a person can be truly heard.

For centuries, psychologists and psychiatrists have recognized the value of the catharsis that occurs when people are able to talk about what's bothering them. To know this, all you have to do is remember the last time you had an issue, and you went to talk with someone about it. They may or may not have offered you advice, but chances are, you said, "Thanks for listening." And, you felt better because you got it off your chest. This common metaphor is describing an actual burden being "lifted" off you.

In many cases, mediation may be the first opportunity someone has had to do this, fully. This is healing. It is curative. It is a gift that mediation provides.

People turn to mediation because they have had a serious conflict they have been unable to resolve. They need structure and guidance. They need a facilitator skilled in handling strong emotion, as well as one who can help uncover and understand the substantive aspects of the conflict. They do not know how to get it over in a way that feels acceptable to them—if they did, they would have done so already.

They need the tools and the emotional support to "get it over."

The mediator enables people to do this by serving as a guide to the process ("getting it going"), delving into the substance in a structured way to uncover interests ("getting it out"), and by providing emotional connection and support ("getting it over"). In other words, the mediator is focused on three aspects: substance, process, and psychology.

The mediator then helps the parties consider options and negotiate, so they can get back to the business of productive work lives.

Consider the neutral phenomenon. Discussion occurs in neutral territory—off-site, away from business premises or outside the office of those involved. This setting neutralizes the subtle power exerted or perceived by virtue of being in someone else's territory. It feels safer.

The mediator has no "skin in the game," but only in the process. Her only goal is to help you deal with conflict, reach a resolution, and help you get to a better place, legally, financially, and emotionally. She is present solely to help you reach that goal. How cool is that?

In mediation, discussions are confidential by law and/or agreement. This adds to a feeling of safety.

Finally, the mediation success process allows the ability to discuss the undiscussable, privately, without judgment. It aids in self-discovery of underlying interests and provides needed emotional support.

The mediator establishes an atmosphere of respectful communication, where questions are asked, and information shared, in a guided, non-confrontational manner.

A person can be angry, she can cry, she can take a break, but always, she can trust the mediator will not let things get out of control. Knowing this allows her to take more risks in sharing information, which in turn leads to greater understanding and ultimately, informed decision-making.

The psychological truth is that people are far more likely to accept suggestions or guidance from a neutral third party. This is because they believe she is objective, and cares. This can be true of any third party—a friend or colleague who is not involved can lend an objective ear. When the third party is one with deep expertise in helping parties solve conflict, people are willing to be even more open and receptive to looking for new ways to get past the tension and the barriers that have been established.

Finally, the mediator is able to remain positive—even when the parties are feeling pessimistic—and persist in looking for unspoken needs and interests and ways to satisfy them.

When the parties have long been mired in conflict and negativity, a positive mediator can help them navigate through and beyond their emotions to settlement.

Working with the emotions, the mediator asks questions to gain clarification, uncovers and shares additional information, and explores options for meeting interests and addressing concerns.

Step 4—Resolve the Conflict

Once the mediator has been able to "get it going," the parties are able to "get it out" so that underlying interests and desires are uncovered. The mediator helps them to "get it over" by ensuring they are fully heard, that their feelings have been validated, and they have been given needed human connection and emotional support.

Once this process has occurred, people are now more open to considering options, negotiating, and resolving the conflict.

Discussions of goals and options for resolution can now begin, with the mediator working to support each person in expressing and meeting as much of their interests as possible, all the while aiming for the "Can Live With" outcome.

In over ten years of mediating, I have made key observations about how people approach resolution in mediation, when it comes time to get down to the business of negotiation. I will share these with you, so you will be able to watch for these actions and respond positively, to increase the chances for successful resolution.

To resolve conflict, and be able to put it behind us, we need to be okay with both the process and the outcome. We feel better when we have fully considered all available information, provided input and made an informed decision. No one imposed it on us; we have no resentment to carry forward, because we agreed on the resolution. Once agreement is reached, the terms are written up and signed by everyone involved.

It's documented in writing. It's been signed. We shook on it. Perhaps hugs were exchanged. We breathed easier, perhaps for the first time in years.

Our dollars no longer need to go towards legal bills. Our time can be spent focusing on productive work. We can start a new job or start a new business.

We have money. Perhaps we have a new feeling of being respected and supported. We have been validated. We finally received that apology or acknowledgement we've been waiting for so long to hear. We have an agreement on confidentiality.

Resolution brings peace and peace restores productivity.

Closing Thoughts:

1. Mediation Success has four steps: Get it Going, Get it Out, Get it Over, and Resolve the Conflict.
2. The first three steps are essential elements of conflict resolution. They set the stage for success, uncover underlying interests, and address deep concerns and emotions that can otherwise block resolution.

PART TWO:

The Process

CHAPTER 4

Get it Going:
Set the Stage for Success

When people sit down with a mediator to resolve conflict, it's not unusual for them to feel frustrated, angry, and worried.

They are most likely pessimistic about the chances of a positive outcome. They know what they want to get out of the mediation, they've thought about it, planned for it, strategized, and are "loaded for bear." They may also be worried, nervous, anxious, and tense. They are almost afraid to hope that this mediator will be able to get them anywhere, or make any progress at all. They may actually be feeling quite vulnerable.

Here is what people are often thinking in their private thoughts:

What if the other person says or does something awful?

What if he is aggressive? What if she yells at me? Can the mediator prevent this from happening or control things if they do?

How on earth is this going to work?

Is this mediator any good? What does she know about conflict, anyway?

Will the mediator truly be able to understand where I am coming from, to empathize with my distress? Do I trust her to get me there?

I am right, the other guy is full of baloney and is wildly unrealistic in his expectations. This mediator better be able to help me get what I want here.

To achieve Mediation Success, the mediator needs to address the "inner game" of conflict. This means he needs to address the negative thoughts that are likely in everyone's mind which serve as barriers to resolution, and in doing so, shift the dynamics.

Open their minds. Create positive thoughts.

Set the Stage for Mediation Success

It is absolutely necessary for the stage to be set for Mediation Success from the outset. If this is done the right way, the mediator can employ all the tools in her toolbox to address situations that might otherwise lead to someone blowing up, walking out, or giving up. The hope is that none of that ever occurs.

In over a thousand mediations, I have never had anyone get angry and storm out. I have had many a mediation where someone has felt as if they wanted to at some point—but it has never happened. That's because I set the stage right at the beginning.

It's up to the conflict resolution professional to do this, and do it right. The parties don't actually have to do anything at this point—just sit, listen, assess the mediator, and agree to some basic ground rules of communication.

That's right, I did say: *"assess the mediator."*

Often, the people involved have not met the mediator before. Make no mistake about it, they have entrusted their well-being, financially and emotionally, to this person for the time-being. They are at mediation because nothing they have done in the past has been able to resolve the situation.

To "Get it Going" and set the stage for success, there are four essential steps, all of which can be accomplished in the first twenty minutes or so.

In the first twenty minutes, you can greatly diffuse tension and increase the odds of resolution. You do this by:

1. Creating rapport
2. Building trust
3. Requesting agreement to three ground rules
4. Revising expectations

1. Create Genuine Rapport

Rapport is essential. Human beings want and need to feel a connection with other people.

To feel that connection, human nature is such that we look to see if we have anything in common with another. We *want* to have something in common. We like others *more* when we feel we share something in common.

Ever wonder why that is? It's because it validates who we are. We believe someone who is "like us" will understand where we are coming from. They might empathize with us; they will understand us.

We want that human connection. Subconsciously, we will have more faith in the mediator if we believe he truly understands us.

Make *extended* introductions. Share as much about yourself, both professionally and personally, as you can in the few minutes you have.

For example, I might start my own introduction this way: "Thank you for selecting me as your mediator. You might have seen some information about me on my website, or heard some information from others, but I thought I'd take a few moments to tell you a bit about myself, so you'll at least have some idea who's sitting with you at the table today."

I tell them I'm a lawyer, and ask them, with a smile, to please not to hold it against me too much.

I tell them how long I've been practicing law "Over 25 years, and please don't start guessing how many more!"

I tell them that my background was in the employment law area and general civil and commercial litigation; that I have a degree in psychology though I certainly don't hold myself out as a psychologist; and that I've been serving as a full-time mediator for ten years or so.

If I have a past relationship with anyone from a prior mediation or otherwise, I talk about it. "I know Mike, and I know Eliot as well. I've worked with each of them several times. It's always good to work with people you have history with—especially good history."

I also tell them about my family. I used to say, "My husband's a lawyer, too. I have three teenagers, including identical twin girls. My day job is much easier than my night job." That often brought a smile. Now, when I talk about my kids, I say, "My son is in college at USC, and my twin daughters are both in college at the University of Denver. Frankly, having survived the teenage years with identical twin girls, there's no conflict I can't handle."

Most people can relate to the fact that it can be quite a challenge to deal with those dynamics, and so that statement often brings a smile as well.

The purpose of sharing this information is two-fold: I want the parties to feel that they are getting to know me, so that they will feel comfortable and be willing to open up with me during the process. In addition, I want to encourage sharing on their part, of not only who they are and what their role is at the mediation, but a bit about themselves professionally and personally.

The goal is uncovering information that might lead someone to feel something they have in common with another. When we find things we share in common, this helps to make a connection that aids in establishing rapport.

Here's an example of how, following an extended introduction by the mediator, the introductions of others frequently go:

"My name is John. I'm an HR generalist from the company. I've been with them four years. This was a new career for me. I used to be an accountant, but it was just too dry for me, and I wanted to deal with people. I have three kids, too, their ages are…."

"I have twins also!" or, "I'm a twin myself."

"I have no kids, but I have two dogs."

"You do? So do I. What kind?"

"I hear Boston in your accent, yes?"

"How did you know?"

"I'm from Boston originally."

"What part? How long ago did you move here?"

"I was in the military for 10 years..."

If we are lucky, we veer off on a tangent or two discussing some aspect of each person. It's like mining for gold.

Each tidbit of information just might open a door to someone else in the room feeling a connection with the mediator, or with another person in the room.

Many mediators do not take the time to go through any sort of extended introduction, based on their desire to get down to it, and their belief that the parties' background is not relevant to the dispute and thus spending time learning this information is a waste of time.

Learning about each other's backgrounds is *not* a waste of time. To the contrary, we aren't talking about the substance of the dispute. This part of the mediation is essential because it recognizes and honors our fundamental human need for connection. This is a key part of the Mediation Success process of conflict resolution.

This stage of the Mediation Success process helps alleviate the anxiety people are likely to be feeling.

2. Build Trust

People want, and need, to trust that you will safely guide them to resolution and ultimately, to peace. When unsure or confused, people in conflict look for that life raft, to give them the hope that resolution is possible.

How can you build that trust? First, establish your credibility.

Recommendations count. If you have been retained privately, presumably you were retained because someone heard good things about your ability to resolve conflict. But, not everyone at the table will have or remember the same information about you. And you may be there because you were appointed, or asked to help, without any input from those involved.

You may be an internal manager or human resource professional that has been asked to step in to help resolve tensions and disputes. A title, such as "ombudsperson" or "company mediator," helps provide instant credibility.

Something about your background, experience, education, or training establishes you as someone who has special expertise in resolving conflict. Share that information. Be sure the people in the room know about this.

Degrees help—in psychology, law, theology, social work, counseling, dispute resolution, and similar fields.

Training and experience resolving conflict, even in a less-formal context, counts.

You might be a former judge, an attorney, a spiritual leader, an employee relations specialist, or just someone who cares.

Share information with those present about the number of mediations you've done, or the number of employees you have helped. Tell them the number of years you have held your position, your background and knowledge in a certain area, or your familiarity with the organization.

Reveal anything that shows you are knowledgeable and experienced. Talk about the percentage of success you have achieved.

Let them know that you've prepared by reviewing all of the information they sent to you ahead of time, or by speaking to someone who retained you about the issues.

Give them a reason to trust that you have special expertise in resolving conflict in general, and their conflict in particular.

Again, like the establishment of genuine rapport, establishing your credibility serves to alleviate the anxiety they are feeling at the moment.

Second, describe the confidential nature of the process. By law in most states, and by agreement in mediation, everything that is said in mediation is confidential. This means that what is said, feelings that are expressed, positions that are taken, negotiations, offers, and responses are all confidential and cannot be used in any kind of a later court or other legal proceeding.

Ask everyone to acknowledge this and sign an agreement to that effect. If you are trying to resolve a workplace dispute or conflict, obtain their agreement not to disclose your discussions to co-workers.

Tell them that you will destroy your notes after the discussions, and that the only "paper" that will remain is any agreement they decide to reach.

Explain that facts and documents that pre-exist aren't made confidential by discussing them, but any comments about them are confidential.

Reassure everyone that if you meet with each of the participants separately, and if there is something they tell you about how they feel or what options they might consider that they wish to remain confidential, that wish will be honored—they simply need to tell you, so you will know.

Once again, you have shared information that will decrease any anxiety they may be feeling due to the risk that something will later "get out" or harm them in the future.

Third, explain the process, and describe your role. Establish yourself as the expert in terms of the process. Explain that the process is designed to be structured but flexible.

Here is what I mean by "structured yet flexible." For example, you meet initially in joint session, where each will be asked to share their "perspective" on what brought them to the table. Then, typically you meet in separate sessions, while "shuttle diplomacy" occurs and the mediator goes back and forth between the parties, obtaining information, asking questions, and exploring options for resolution.

However, sometimes problem-solving occurs while in joint session and there may be no need to break into separate session. At other times, the mediator might want to meet separately with the lawyers, or even (with the lawyer's permission, of course) with the parties.

Once in separate session, there might be a desire to get together again jointly, to ask questions or work together on a certain aspect of resolution, or to facilitate an apology.

Explain what your role is and how it fits into the process. It's important that you describe your role so that people know what you do and how you can help.

The mediator's role is to do the following:

1. Facilitate communication and negotiation
2. Provide information
3. Help generate options for resolution
4. Play "devil's advocate" if anyone appears to be clinging strongly to a position without giving consideration to other potentially reasonable ways to view the situation

When explaining your first role, which is "to facilitate communication and negotiation," reassure the parties that strong emotions, such as anxiety and even anger, are normal. Here, they appreciate the fact that what they are feeling is normal and that you have thus provided some needed validation.

Sometimes when I say that strong emotions, such as anxiety, anger, or fear, are normal, I see tears appear in someone's eyes. Why the tears? Because they are grateful that someone understands how they are feeling.

When talking about strong emotion, it is worth stating that it is common for someone's adrenaline to get going, which is *perfectly acceptable*. This statement usually surprises everyone, because they believe they should not display emotion and certainly shouldn't "lose it" and become argumentative.

It is important, though, to explicitly state that the display of strong emotion is "perfectly acceptable—*unless* I perceive that the adrenaline or emotion has risen to such a level that it might be blocking them from getting where they want to go, which is resolving their conflict."

You can explain that, if you perceive that might be occurring, you might suggest breaking into separate session, or might step outside with them privately, so that you can hear and learn more about what's going on for them at that time. Explain that you want to be able to address their concerns, if possible, so that they can set those strong feelings aside and help them make progress toward resolution.

The above information is hugely reassuring. People are often afraid that the other person, or they themselves, might "lose it" by crying or yelling, and escalate the conflict. They need to know you can handle displays of strong emotion, and trust that you will deal with the situation and bring it back under control if it does.

This approach provides the reassurance—and hence, the trust—that you can handle strong emotion and will ensure that it will not serve as a barrier to resolution.

Mediation Success Rule #4:
Language is key to setting the stage for success, so use words that reduce anxiety and build trust.

Selective language is part of the Mediation Success process. Words are chosen purposefully, each designed to set the stage for Mediation Success.

By describing the process as "structured, yet flexible" you make everyone aware that you know the process, and are in charge of the structure. You are confident. You are so in charge, in fact, that you know that it's okay to be flexible, and will do whatever is needed to "flex" the process that will advance the progress towards resolution.

You know what to do. This is greatly reassuring.

By telling each person that what they feel is "normal" and "acceptable," you provide validation. They no longer need to expend emotional energy trying *not* to feel nervous or anxious, or trying to hide those potentially embarrassing emotions.

They appreciate that you understand and empathize with how they are feeling. You have established a connection, and lifted a burden from their shoulders.

By telling them what you will do if you "perceive" that strong emotions "might" be interfering with progress, you are reassuring them that you will be paying attention, not only to what is being said, but to what may be going on with them emotionally, and that you will hop to their aid if there is any serious risk of those emotions getting in their way.

Finally, by describing what you will do—facilitate, generate, provide, play the role of devil's advocate—in active terms, you are telling them you will play an active part in working to help solve the conflict. You are not going to simply sit there and listen, but you will be rolling up your sleeves to work with them to reach resolution.

Words that Encourage Trust:

Structured
Flexible
Normal
Acceptable
Perceive
Might
Facilitate
Generate
Provide
Play the Role of Devil's Advocate

3. Ask for Agreement to Three Requests

There are a few basic ground rules that must be agreed to, to keep the process respectful. Ask everyone if they would be willing to agree to three requests, which will become the basis for respectful ground rules for discussion.

1.   To refer to each other on a first name basis.
2.   To allow each other to say, fully and completely, whatever it is they have to say, without interruption.
3.   To fully disclose anything and everything you feel is important.

What are the reasons for these requests?

Refer to each other on a first name basis. When people are in conflict, they tend to de-personalize each other, and refer to the other as "he" or "she" or "the plaintiff" or "my client." When someone is referred to in that way, he will tend to feel somewhat defensive. A first-name basis rule helps to take the formality down a bit. It also helps diffuse the anger that people may feel.

This explanation usually generates nods and agreement. Sometimes, though, there is opposition, due to cultural differences. For example, southerners often have a strong desire to use the titles of "Mr." or "Mrs." It's ingrained in them as a matter of respect. The same can be true with disputes between staff and physicians. They use "Dr. Smith" out of habit and respect.

Remember "structured, yet flexible"? In that case, since it's meant as a sign of respect, respect trumps. Go with it.

Allow each other to say, fully and completely, whatever it is they have to say, without interruption. Most people understand that listening, without interruption, is respectful. Aside from being respectful, there are some added practical reasons for this request as well.

It is actually more efficient for each person to say their piece, sequentially.

When we are interrupted, two things happen. We become irritated with the person who interrupts us. And, we tend (at least I do) to forget what it was we were going to say. So, you want to be sure that doesn't happen.

It's important to establish, and maintain, a respectful environment that allows each person to feel heard. Being fully heard is essential to a successful mediation. First and foremost, "venting" can bring the catharsis that can be so essential to allowing us to move forward. Obtaining agreement to allowing each person to speak fully removes the fear people may fear about not being able to get it all out.

Mediation Success Rule #5:
Being fully heard is essential to any mediation.

Fully disclose anything and everything that they feel is important. A critical part of conflict resolution is allowing full expression of whatever information each side believes the other needs to know—whether it's factual information, or information about how that person feels, or the impact that a conflict has had on their professional or personal life.

Explain that, in a moment, everyone will be invited to share their perspective about what it is that brought them to the table.

When I get to this point, I offer that I use the word "perspective" intentionally. This is because we come to the table knowing where we are coming from and perhaps assuming we know where the other side is coming from, but typically we don't know the full story.

I stress that, when we tell a story about something that has happened, we tend to tell it as if it is fact. In reality, it's usually a blend—of fact, of what we recall, of what we believe, of what we've been told by our friends, colleagues or lawyers, and of how we feel.

I offer also, "That's all perfectly legitimate. It all simply makes up our perspective. And, again, while we know where we come from, we don't know where the other side is coming from."

I continue: "What happens in mediation is that new information is learned. I never know what that new information is going to be. It could be a fact, a document you hadn't seen, a statement someone made you didn't know. It could be something about the legal aspect of your claim or defense. It might be information that I can provide as the mediator. Or, it could be something as simple as how one of you feels about which the other was not aware.

"While I don't know what the new information will be, I do know that this information generally opens the door to resolution, where it might not have been possible before."

Remember the emotional stages? Exchanging full information is critical to get to the awareness stage. It's that new information we are looking for, that has not been shared or known previously. When parties are allowed to talk, unscripted and uninterrupted, you would be amazed at what comes out. Awareness of new information hopefully leads to the acknowledgement ("I didn't know that before. This is news to me!") and ultimately, a new analysis of how that new information impacts their choices and thoughts about resolution.

Mediation Success Rule #6:
Word choice matters, so choose words that help bridge differences.

Key Words:

Perspective
Story
Legitimate
Allow
Fully
Disclose
New

As with building trust, language is key and word choice matters.

"Perspective" and "story" indicate there is not only one true or factual way to describe what happened in any given conflict. While there are facts, there are also memories, feelings, and input from others that impact how we view the situation, and what we are willing to do.

Obtaining acknowledgement of the existence of different perspectives, before anyone has jumped into the substance, opens the door to resolution by opening the mind from a past fixation to the "truth" as one knows it to be, to the potential that there may be another way someone else can reasonably view the same circumstances. The acknowledgement is typically non-verbal here. I see heads nodding, which is all I need to see.

"Legitimate" tells each person that they are justified, and hence validated, in seeing the situation the way they do and feeling as they do—at that moment in time, based on all the factors that come into play. This statement of "legitimacy" has the effect of relieving people of the burden of spending precious emotional energy to establish the righteousness of their beliefs.

"Allow" causes the parties to feel magnanimous. They are not being told they *have to* listen to the other side. They agree, by choice, to allow the other to speak, and in the process enable themselves to be open to hearing new information.

Choice is good. And, they have made this decision themselves. They hear and understand the reason for the request, they have nodded or expressed assent, and have opened their mind to the possibility of hearing something new that just might influence them to re-evaluate their position.

"Fully" means no secrets. No one wants to be sandbagged and then feel they have been cheated, which will make them want to undo an agreement. Each wants to feel they are making a fully informed decision. No one wants to continue in intense and expensive and emotionally draining conflict, only to learn years later information which, had they known, would have motivated them to resolve the conflict at the time.

"Disclose" imposes an obligation on the parties that they voluntarily agree to. Disclosure of anything that's important to someone is essential, because everyone should be aware that people resolve conflict in mediation for all sorts of reasons—legal and non-legal, personal, financial, business, emotional—and the more the mediator and the other people involved know about what's important to them, the better able each will be to help meet their needs and resolve the conflict. In other words: the greater the likelihood there will be mediation *success*.

"New" in regards to information, provides two essential keys of Mediation Success. First, it provides a rational reason for someone to analyze his position differently. Second, it provides the dignity essential to changing one's position, when one has steadfastly refused to do so in the past.

4. Revise Expectations

If you tell someone, "you need to change your expectations," they will resist. This is even more true if you tell them, "you need to *lower* your expectations."

"Why should I do that? Absolutely not!" would be the expected response.

Yet, there are two key expectations that need to be changed for Mediation Success to occur: the expectation that resolution will not occur, and the expectation that they will get the outcome they planned for (i.e, they will "win").

People in mediation are often pessimistic about resolution. And why not? The tension has reached a place where it's so disruptive they have had to turn to a third party; they have not been able to resolve it themselves. Why should they have any reason to think the matter will settle, or relationships will improve?

But, if people are not optimistic, why would they invest significant effort in working towards a solution? Positive thinking is the key.

Mediation Success Rule #7:
Revise expectations! Create optimism and encourage realism with the "Can Live With" goal.

Create Optimism

The goal here is to instill hope that resolution is not only possible, but likely. Here is an example of how to do this:

> Before we begin getting into the substance of why we're here, I'd like to share with you that in my experience, well over 90% of the time we reach resolution through this process. While that's not a guarantee, those are pretty good odds, if you stick with me here.

This information shifts the mind, ever so slightly, to have hope that progress will be made. Human nature is that if we feel we have no hope, we give up. If we have hope, we keep plugging towards achieving our goal, in this case, resolution.

Create Realism

Go for the "Can live with-can live with" outcome. Remember the story at the beginning of this book about the CEO who said, "Isn't mediation about winning?" "No," I told him, "It's about resolution."

It's important for everyone to know that mediation is about reaching an agreement that puts the matter behind you, so you can get it out, get it over, and get back to business.

Expecting to be ecstatic about a huge "win" is not what the process of mediation is directed towards. But how do you change the mindset of one who is not prepared to give up such a goal? By explaining the key concept of the Mediation Success approach: the goal of the "Can Live With-Can Live With" outcome. Simply providing this information is enough to accomplish this change is viewpoint.

I typically do this by comparing and contrasting the processes of going to court (litigation) and mediation. Here is how I do it:

> If you are familiar with the court system, that's a "win-lose" approach to conflict, right? One side wins, one side loses. People who are familiar with mediation often call it "win-win," and I've heard lawyers call it "lose-lose." I have a different view of mediation. I call it, "Can live with — can live with."

> People generally don't dance out of mediation ecstatically happy. More often, they say, "Well, okay, perhaps this is not the outcome I envisioned before I came here today, but all things considered, now that I've had a chance to look at this from additional perspectives, this is an outcome I can live with, which brings me the peace that comes with resolution."

> Because I find that goal to be realistic, and reachable, that is my goal for you and for this process today.

I have never once made this statement, where I did not see small smiles of acknowledgement and heads nodding.

They *get it*. They have now opened their mind to the possibility of resolution, in a way different from what they have wanted or insisted upon in the past, by realizing that there may be another outcome they can live with, and get the peace that comes with resolution.

Closing Thoughts

1. Everyone wants peace. They want to stop the tension, stop the financial and emotional drain, the drain on productivity.

2. They need to "get it out" and "get it over," so they can "get back to business" by agreeing on a resolution, improving the relationship, and returning to a productive life, personally and professionally.
3. Mediation Success requires setting the stage by creating rapport, building trust, obtaining agreement to simple ground rules, and revising expectations.

Now, you have learned how to successfully "get it going." You have set the stage for success by creating the environment necessary for the full sharing of perspectives.

The parties have begun to feel a connection with you, to trust that you know what you are doing, that you can handle the emotional aspects of the conflict, that you will not be judgmental, and that you will do what it takes to enable them to get to the business of resolution.

You are now ready to dig deep. Let's see what true underlying interests can be revealed when we invite people to "get it out."

CHAPTER 5

Get Around the Obstacles: Myths of Mediation

Mediation Success means resolving the conflict at hand. To do this, the mediator needs to be aware of the psychological factors that are attendant to negotiation. While lots of books have been written about how to negotiate to "win," the goal of a mediator is to help parties "resolve."

In mediation, the business of resolution involves negotiation. Negotiation implies back and forth efforts to "win," not to resolve. Yet, resolving the conflict is the key to returning to the business of your company, and the business of living.

Knowing that, it is important to be mindful that the end goal of negotiation in mediation is not to win: it is to resolve.

Go for the "Can Live With" Outcome

A key piece of advice is to be realistic.

It's critical for parties to know that the court process is a "win/lose" proposition. One side wins, and one side loses. The business of negotiation in mediation involves helping parties to voluntarily reset their expectations, from a "win" to a realistic "can live with" outcome.

It helps to know that several commonly-held beliefs are in reality, myths.

As discussed in earlier chapters, people generally don't leave mediation ecstatically happy, feeling that they "won." Rather, they leave with a feeling of ultimate success that they were able to achieve peace.

The Can Live With-Can Live With outcome is realistic. It is perceived as reachable by both parties. Can Live With-Can Live With should be the goal of the mediator and of those who are in conflict.

I tell my mediation clients that this outcome is my goal for them and for this process.

That choice is empowering. Their decision is an educated choice, based on consideration of all sorts of varied information they had not had, or had not been able, to consider before. We may have started meeting at 9 a.m., and it may be late in the afternoon, when I hear someone say, "Fine. I can live with that." When we reach that point, the person will look at me, smile, and say, "Aha!"

Assuming these words resonate with those in the room (and they usually do), this statement of philosophy acts as a "reset." It redefines expectations, and changes the definition of a positive outcome where one "wins" by getting everything they planned for, to where one "wins" (i.e., feels better) by making an informed decision about what, in fact, they are willing to "live with" to put this conflict behind them, and move on with life.

Negotiation success, and as a result, Mediation Success, increases when expectations are voluntary set at a more realistic level.

Myths and Misconceptions of Negotiations in Mediation

As part of resolving conflict in mediation, it helps to know that several commonly-held beliefs are in reality, myths.

Myth #1: People Mean What They Say
Reality: Absolute Statements are Expressions of Current Intent

Most of us believe that people mean what they say. However, what I've come to know is that people do *not* always mean what they say, when faced with serious conflict. Or at least, not initially. Eventually, they may get there.

It's not that they are lying. They may just be strategizing. What they are telling you is part of their "negotiation" plan. They may be trying to see if they can get away with "not telling the whole truth." And, if they are not quite telling the whole truth, usually they will, eventually.

Knowing that statements of what someone is willing to do or not do is all part of strategy, I never assume initial statements of positions, authority, goals, or even facts, are accurate.

The key for a conflict-resolver is not to make judgments or assign negative attributes to someone who is not being totally straightforward. Realize instead that human nature is to try to get the best possible resolution for oneself, and as a result, people will take positions that they believe will help them reach the ultimate goal.

Let me give some examples. The following statement was in a letter I received from a lawyer before the mediation:

"If they don't open with at least $100,000, we will take that as bad faith and will immediately leave the mediation."

I thought, "Uh-oh. I am going to take this as an expression of a desire that the other side start at $100,000. That's a pretty high number to start with, in my experience. If he is serious, I wonder if the other side is aware of this. Perhaps the lawyer wrote that more for his client's benefit. At any rate, I'd better make a phone call to see if there is a significant risk of this mediation going south in the first 30 minutes."

If this statement was true, the process was in trouble, and I needed to alert the other side, early. However, I decided to check. I called the lawyer. He told me he made this statement, because he and his client recalled having verbal conversations with the other side, where they had informally discussed $100,000 as an offer. The attorney told me the threat to leave was an expression of his client's desire. He confided, though, that his client had an unrealistic evaluation of what his case was worth and told me he would appreciate my help at the mediation in educating his client about some of the factors that affect what a terminated employee may be likely to recover.

At the mediation, negotiations began at $25,000. The case ultimately settled at less than $100,000. Clearly, the lawyer did not mean what he said.

Be wary of absolute statements. Sometimes one side says, "We can't pay more than $X amount," or "My bottom line is $X." Their statement is absolute, so the other party believes that the other side meant what they've said.

The myth is that a party "can't" do something. The reality is that "can't" most often means, "don't want to" or "not willing to." The absolute statement must be tested.

What one is willing to do is influenced by several factors. One factor is how far apart the parties are from one another. If after protracted negotiations, the parties are not too far apart, they can "taste it" and realize their suffering may soon be over. It is amazing how many times I've heard "Fine. Let's do it," after someone has repeated many times that they "absolutely can't" accept what the other side is willing to offer.

My informal rule is that someone needs to say "no" three times before I believe them.

That's because I take absolute statements as mere attempts to convey how serious someone is about what it is they want. I do my best to dissuade someone from using words that can paint them into a corner where they will lose credibility and no longer be able to negotiate with integrity if they move again.

Mediation Success Rule #8:
Get "no" 3 times before you accept a statement as a true indicator of position.

Even if they do mean no, if they are saying something that early in the process, they are basing it on a pre-mediation evaluation that does not reflect any new information they may learn in the process. If they do mean it, I know that is their "bottom line"—but only for the moment. I will do my best either to work with them privately on how to communicate their position and still leave the door open, or, I will reword the communication myself, in accordance with my knowledge that there is more room, my belief that there may be more room, or even my unfounded hope there may be more.

Only when I am firmly convinced they really, really aren't moving, will I communicate it as such. In that case, if an impasse looms, I often will continue the negotiations over the coming weeks.

People will lie to protect themselves. Sometimes, when a person is afraid that the truth will be devastating, he will do everything possible to hide the truth. He may make statements that he really does not mean, or knows are untrue, and will stick to them.

One of the key roles of the conflict-resolver is to help someone in distress about the impact of his actions on his future by helping him to understand that, although it may seem as if hiding the truth is the way to go for self-preservation, the ultimate damage which occurs from the fall-out of a lie is often far greater than the admission of improper behavior.

Extend the gift of understanding that it is natural to be guarded about the truth initially, that you understand how difficult it is for them, and you, at least, will not judge and will do all you can to help minimize the impact of the admission. The combination of empathy, persistence, and lack of moral judgment will often provide the dignified opening a person needs to "come clean."

In one circumstance, I was asked by a company to conduct an investigation into whether an executive had sexually harassed a young woman we'll call Sara who worked for him. She had resigned, and in doing so, told the company human resource director, "I'm not going to sue, but I just want you to know that Harry pursued me for three months, trying to get an intimate relationship going with me. Eventually he stopped. I didn't care, but then when I wanted to apply for a new position that would be a promotion, reporting to him, he told me not to, that it wouldn't be a good idea. I realized I needed to leave so I found another job. I just wanted you to know."

The human resource director knew that she was required to investigate and asked Harry about the accusation. When asked about pursuing Sara, Harry denied it. Company phone records revealed he had placed numerous calls to Sara, after business hours. Harry said all the calls were "for business purposes." The company CEO asked him about it, too, and Harry continued to insist everything was on the "up and up."

So, by the time I was engaged to investigate, Harry had already been interviewed, twice.

The very first thing Harry said to me was, "I'm happily married. I've been married for 25 years, so I would never do such a thing."

I said, "Harry, I didn't ask you about your marriage. I asked you if you pursued Sara for an intimate relationship."

"I did not."

"Are you sure? These phone records seem to tell a different story."

"I'm sure. I told you, I've been married for 25 years."

I took a breath, and looked him directly in the eye. "Harry—I'm not meaning to offend you, but I don't know you, we've only just met today. What I've come to know is that, in my experience, the fact that someone has been married for a long time does not necessarily have any bearing on whether they may have made overtures to another person. It may actually mean the opposite! No judgment, Harry—I won't think you are a bad person. I just need to know the truth. Because if the truth is different from what you've said, and it comes out in some other type of proceeding, I'm not sure you would want that. "

Silence. I waited. More silence. Then, the confession: "I did, I did call her, several times. I was traveling and it was a rocky period in my marriage. I never touched her, ever; I only tried to get her to go out with me, but after a time when she wasn't interested, I stopped. Are you going to tell my wife?"

I replied that of course, I would not, as it was not my place to do so. I told him that I did, however, need to tell his employer.

As a person who is accustomed to people not always being completely truthful, I have trained myself to be both patient and non-judgmental or at least to suspend any judgment relating to the lack of truthfulness. I simply persist in the process.

Myth #2: We Can Do Better Than The Last Offer
Reality: The Last Offer May No Longer Be on the Table

People prepare for negotiation in mediation based on their knowledge of past negotiations and where they left off, believing that is the logical place to start. Often, though, a party appears at mediation with a different position—a lower offer or a higher demand—than was discussed in the months prior.

In legal cases, past offers, whether verbal or in writing, are not binding if they are not accepted. That means that anyone can change their mind about what they may be willing to do to resolve a dispute, and even completely withdraw an offer. This dynamic can happen even within the mediation itself.

Whether in a legal case, or in a business negotiation, this situation leads to bad feelings and an accusation that the other is acting in bad faith. That's because, psychologically, it's hard to unring the bell.

The reality is that statements made verbally are subject to differing recall. It may be that the other side honestly has no recollection of ever making a past verbal offer and thus feels no compulsion to start there.

Also, at times verbal offers are made without real authority, but only to test the waters. What one person remembers as a firm verbal offer, another recalls as only discussion of a "possibility". ("If I could get my client to pay $100,000, would your client accept that?")

Other times, circumstances have changed since the verbal offers were made, and so a party is not willing to start there. In one recent situation, a company had offered an employee a transfer as a possible resolution many months earlier. It turned out that by the time the mediation was held, the position had been filled and so was no longer available as an option.

Finally, if much time has passed since a resolution was discussed, it is fair to assume that expenses have increased, legal fees have been incurred, or more time has been lost from work.

So, to fully prepare, don't assume anything about where the other person may be coming from—where they will start or where they will end up. (You know what they say about what happens when you assume.)

Myth #3: They Won't Change Their Mind
Reality: People Change Their Minds

People take positions based on a set of known circumstances. But then, life happens! Circumstances change.

Financial situations may alter, so that a person who has brought a claim may end up needing money sooner, rather than later. An employee may get a better job and as a result does not care to drag out the stress and tension any longer.

A newly-divorced spouse may meet someone new, with different financial circumstances. Perhaps someone's basis for emotional support is changed.

A serious fact not to be taken lightly is this: we get worn out by extended conflict. New information becomes available, which causes employees or companies to view outcomes that initially seemed unpalatable, as potentially reasonable.

Businesses have a need to move on—or they may be affected by the economy.

The reality is that our minds are not static, but are always in a state of dynamic evaluation. Time goes on, and, if the mediator stays in touch, often one or both parties will in fact change their mind.

Myth #4: If It Can't Be Resolved Today, It Never Will Be Resolved
Reality: Resolution Is Always Possible

It is true that the best time to achieve resolution is at the mediation. This is because people are there, physically present and mentally focused on one thing: resolution. Once they return to work and their lives, other distractions and influences can derail the process.

Often, a person believes that resolution is simply not possible because everyone gave it their best effort already. It's important not to give up. As long as someone who is invested in the process stays with it, a safe zone is created for parties to change their positions. Even a slight move can help the process.

Relationships develop and discussions can continue. I have observed that the relationships that I develop with the people in conflict, or their lawyers, allow for more candid discussions than would otherwise occur.

Persistence is essential. In one particularly complex matter, at the mediation itself, based on the information presented, I believed the case should resolve at a certain dollar figure. The parties had taken wildly extreme positions (an opening demand of $13 million, down to $9 million at the end of the session, and a closing offer at the end of the day of $400,000.) I shared my thoughts with each side privately that day, but my opinion was not universally accepted and so we parted ways for the day.

Afterwards, I spoke almost daily with the lawyers for each side for about six weeks. We were all in different parts of the country and had other work to do. Yet, we kept at it.

Ultimately, between discussions and e-mail, we got it done. Persistence, patience and optimism increased the odds for resolution. And guess what it resolved for? The very number I thought it would, six weeks earlier.

Myth #5: A Court Will Hear the Truth and Justice Will Prevail
Reality: There is No Guarantee the "Truth" Will Lead to Justice

People become very angry when they learn that someone denies making a statement they know was made. They will use inflammatory words, like "bad faith" and "lying."

The fact is, we frequently have differing recollections of an event or a conversation. Yet, we will insist they know what was said to us. So, when accused of making a statement we are sure we did not make, it is not unusual to immediately become defensive and go on the attack. We take it personally.

"Are you calling me a liar?" is an often-expressed objection.

Most people who are not experienced with the legal process believe that if they only get their day in court, the truth will come out and deserved justice will be theirs.

In the legal arena, the truth does not exist in and of itself. It must be proven. What's important to be aware of is that the judge or jury may not believe one person's version. In other words, the truth is whatever the judge or jury says it is—not what the one person knows it to be.

That can be a hard reality to grasp. If there is no incontrovertible proof, such as a memo or a video, the situation can become a "he said/she said" situation, which means it's anyone's guess as to how the "truth" will be determined by a judge or jury.

I've learned it is a waste of time to try and convince someone that things did not occur as they recall. Rather, it's important to educate people about the fact that there is a dispute—that they have different recollections—and ultimately, a judge or jury will decide which version they believe.

It's not about the truth—it's about what a third person will conclude most likely happened. Understanding this often helps refocus the analysis from a more objective point of view.

The belief that justice will certainly prevail is also a myth. There is no absolute guarantee. Not only must a person convince the trier of fact that her version of the facts are true, but she also must be sure that the judge or jury will apply the law to the facts correctly.

Judges are human too, and they can make mistakes. That is the reason for Courts of Appeal. And, courts and legislators can change the law.

The long and short is that, unfortunately, there are no guarantees that justice will prevail.

Actually, there is no short. It's only long. It takes years for a legal matter to wend its way through the court system. Ever heard the phrase, "Justice delayed is justice denied?" Delay is inevitable. Attorneys file motions, witnesses move away or forget important facts, and other cases get in the way and cause postponements of the long-anticipated day in court.

Knowing the reality, the mediator can help educate each person and so help them to evaluate their positions in light of what may be greater uncertainty than they imagined at the outset.

Myth #6: The Mediator Has the Right Answer
Reality: The Mediator Does Not Make the Decision

While people certainly want a mediator who is experienced in conflict resolution, they also want a mediator who is neutral. The mediator is not personally involved and will not look at the situation the same way a party will. There will be no personal impact on the mediator. So, parties to a conflict often believe that the mediator is the all-knowing conflict guru and will provide the right answer at the end of the day.

The mediator may have suggested alternatives or solutions for the parties to consider. The mediator's neutrality, though, does not mean the mediator has the one right or "fair" solution. The mediator has not lived with the conflict and may not know all the relevant factors that influence a party's thinking.

This is because what seems fair to the mediator may not feel fair to the person hearing it. Once a solution is expressed as "fair" by the mediator, he runs the risk of losing credibility as a neutral from anyone who does not have the same perspective. Resistance might develop which will negatively impact the connection between the mediator and the party.

For this reason, the best approach for the mediator who is asked early on what they think is fair: "It's a bit early to say. I'm not sure what a reasonable outcome might be at this point. You can determine that, but certainly let's keep working towards a reasonable range."

The ultimate answer will be the answer of the parties, not the mediator. They can, and will, arrive at that point with the mediator's assistance.

Whether partners should stay together, whether an employee should seek a new position or strive for departure with dignity, or how much a company should pay is a decision to be made by each person after they have become as fully informed as possible about all the factors that are relevant.

The solution is then their own, and they will be at a far greater place of peace when the decision is theirs, as compared to a solution generated by another and imposed upon them.

For this reason, it is far better for the mediator to withhold offering opinions until she is fairly confident all the important information has been shared. Remember, an opinion is only that: an opinion, which is always subject to change.

Closing Thoughts

1. For Mediation Success, the conflict-resolver and the people in conflict all need to be aware of the myths and misconceptions routinely held about how others negotiate, and what will occur in the future if they do not resolve the matter.

2. People in conflict take positions, seeking to act in what they perceive to be their own best interests, based only on what they know at that moment.

3. A wise mediator, and a great mediation teacher, James Melamed, once said, "All behavior is motivated by positive intent. That positive intent may just be towards themselves." This insight can lead to creative ways to negotiate to meet the interests of each person.

PART THREE:

The Psychology

CHAPTER 6

Get it Out: Reach the Real Issue

When it comes time to actually delve into the substance of the conflict, what's really important is getting to the "it" that needs to be shared.

The "it" is the real issue. It is the root cause of the tension. It is the underlying desire that is escalating the conflict because it is not being met.

In order to have Mediation Success, what needs to be known is the true underlying desire or need that's not being met. Why is that person so angry? Why have they been so unreasonable? Why can't they simply get past this conflict, and move on?

In figuring out the answer to this question, I learned much by listening to people speak in mediation. Rarely does the real issue come out in the first five minutes. Indeed, they may not even be aware themselves of what the heart of the conflict really is until they get into it and start speaking, at length, in a safe environment. Only then, does the true interest or desire emerge.

Getting It Out: How to Uncover the Driving Force

Mediation Success is achieved by understanding the underlying interests and the driving forces lying at the heart of the person's anger and frustration.

It's vitally important, therefore, for the manager, mediator, or human resource manager to be sure that enough time is allowed for each person to speak, uninterrupted, when they are invited to share their perspective.

Remember, it is the new information that often opens the door to resolution, where it might not have been possible before. That "new information" may well be the true underlying interest or need, which was not known before. This is best shared, and explained, by the person himself, because he will have the accompanying emphasis that will make the most impact. "Getting it out" has the most value when it's shared not only with the neutral facilitator, but with the other party as well. For this reason, it is best if as much discussion as possible can be done initially in joint session.

Getting it out has the most value when done face-to-face, in joint session.

Sometimes people are simply not comfortable talking extensively in joint session. In that case, the next step is to meet with each person privately, being sure again to allow sufficient time. Be patient, and encouraging. Wait. Eventually, they talk.

Often, I find that no sooner are we behind closed doors, in separate session, than a person immediately starts unloading with all sorts of information he had not felt comfortable sharing with others present.

If there's not enough time on the first day for full exploration, set a separate time in the future to meet again, as soon as possible.

Remember, people must trust that you will not be judgmental, will keep information confidential if asked to, and will work to address their true concerns.

If you believe there may be "more" that's not being shared, ask, "What is this about for you?" "Are there any other concerns that you haven't shared?" "Is there anything else that's important to you?"

Here are the keys steps to helping someone to "get it out."

1. Tell them you will soon be asking them to share their perspective about what brought them to you today.
2. Share your knowledge that "perspective" is made up of all sorts of things: facts, what you recall, what you believe, how you feel, what you've heard, and what your family, friends, colleagues, or lawyers have told you, and that this is all perfectly legitimate, it just makes up each person's perspective.

3. Explain that people resolve conflicts for all sorts of reasons: legal, financial, practical, business, or emotional reasons, and that all of that is okay.

4. Stress how important it is that each person fully disclose anything and everything that is important to them. Full disclosure is important because there are two things most people don't want to see happen:

    a. They don't resolve their conflict. Months or years pass. Trial occurs, or things escalate to the point where someone leaves the company. Later, they learn a fact that is so important that, had they known it at the time of mediation, they might have resolved things right then and there—and not have had to go through all the time, aggravation and expense of the conflict. "If they had only told me!"

    b. They *do* resolve their conflict, and later, learn about a fact or a piece of information that is so important, if they had known, they never would have resolved things, or at least not the way they did.

No one wants those outcomes to happen.

The only way to ensure they do not is for each person to agree to be fully forthcoming about anything they feel is important. Agreed?

Mediation Success Rule #9:
Invite each person to share their perspective.

Allow plenty of time for each to be fully heard.
Be patient.
Be persistent.
Be focused.
Listen well.
Paraphrase, summarize, reflect, clarify.
Ask again.
Stay with it until you get to the driving force of the desire.

The Real "IT": The Driving Force of Desires

Parties and their lawyers who come to mediation state what they "want." Frequently, they plan a strategy of negotiating, in order to get what they want.

Other times, there is no formal strategy—the person simply steadfastly clings to what he or she wants. And the parties typically assume it's all about money—getting as much as possible, paying as little as possible.

I will never forget a lawyer's comment, made to me in a mediation: "It's *always* about money!"

And yet, in my experience, it's not just about dollars.

What I have found as a mediator of employment and commercial disputes is that, though the demand for resolution often is made in terms of money, in reality, different desires underlie the demand and serve as the true motivation, and hence, the "driving force." We are all driven by desire. In mediation, the strongest desire is the deep underlying need that compels us to push, fight and resist resolution until that need is acknowledged and met. Notably, we may not even be aware of what our strongest desire really is until the process begins and we start speaking about what happened and expressing how we truly feel.

The desire for money is typically tied to a need for compensation and/or financial security. An employee or executive who has lost his or her job needs income, as well as, perhaps, insurance and other fringe benefits. There may be a need to be able to obtain new employment. An employer that does not have unlimited financial resources does not want to erode the foundation of its business. A company also wants to avoid undue publicity that could lead to other employees filing claims and more financial exposure.

The desire for money is a very real need that exists in many, if not most, cases. Yet there can be, and often are, additional strong desires that drive the mediation process. Resolution is often blocked until such desires are addressed.

What follows is a list of nine key desires that I have seen emerge consistently as the driving force in resolution of employment and business conflict. To illustrate, here are some examples from actual mediations.

1. The Desire To Be Heard

Sometimes, an employee is told the reason for adverse employment action such as a transfer, demotion or termination—but feels that he or she was not given a true opportunity to respond. Typically, only non-exempt employees in the government setting have a true "due process" right to both notice and "the opportunity to be heard." There is no corresponding right in the private sector, unless it has been previously negotiated in a contract. Yet it doesn't feel fair if someone just decides we are "out," without hearing our side of the story.

> "I just needed them to hear what I had to say. They never even asked me for the explanation. I tried to explain but they wouldn't listen."
> —A terminated manager

> "I complained, but the company didn't take me seriously, and did nothing to change the situation. It's been over a year and this is the first time I've had a chance to tell my story."
> —A woman who filed a sexual harassment charge because no one would listen to her

Even when a case is in litigation, being deposed may not fulfill the employee's desire to be heard. Answering questions in a stressful "Q&A" environment while under oath and instructed by their lawyer only to answer "yes" or "no" or "I don't recall" is not the same as actually having the ability to speak freely about what happened and how he or she feels.

Everyone has a fundamental need to be "heard." One does not need to be a trained psychologist to know that we all simply feel better when we have the chance to vent, and someone actually listens to us. Where there is a strong desire to be heard, or a need for catharsis, that desire will be the driving force. Resolution is stalled until that need is met.

2. The Desire for Acknowledgment and Apology

The desire for acknowledgment and apology are closely related, and they follow on the heels of the desire to be heard. Often, one party wants the other to verbally indicate that they "get it"—they understand. Most of us believe that if someone who has offended us is made to understand the damage they have caused, that person will apologize.

Two of the most powerful words in the English language, and in mediation, are "I'm sorry." Often one side cannot bring himself to say the words, or he might insist, "I did not do anything wrong, and I am not going to apologize."

The need for apology is so deep, and so universal in conflict, that it is recognized in some states that offer statutory protection for those who extend apologies, such as physicians in malpractice actions. In mediation, expressions of apology or regret are protected from disclosure in any subsequent proceeding, should the matter not resolve.

"She has no idea of the impact her quitting had on this company. She has no idea of the sacrifice I made in terms of the hours I had away from my family, on airplanes, out of town for weeks on end for a full year! Cleaning up the mess, figuring things out on my own, hiring a replacement. I am still dealing with the aftermath."
—A party, suing on a breach of an employment contract

"All I wanted was an apology. It's not about the money, truly. If they had only apologized, I never would have brought this lawsuit. I feel better now, I truly do."
— An employee who, denied commissions, finally received the needed acknowledgment.

The other key point about apologies is this: Apologies typically generate reciprocal behavior. In other words, they generate one of two responses:
1. A reciprocal apology: "That's OK, thanks. I, too, apologize for my role in escalating the matter."
2. Deep gratitude: "Thanks. I appreciate that."

The apology meets the need for acknowledgment, implicitly asks for forgiveness, and allows the person to grant that forgiveness or incorporate the acknowledgment, and thus, to heal and move on. Once that need is met, the door is opened for resolution.

In a recent case, I sensed that the parties could not move on until they believed the other truly realized the impact on each other's lives of the events of the underlying case. With the lawyers' permission, I asked both parties to meet with me alone, without their lawyers, for a facilitated discussion. Though anxious about doing so, they agreed. Both cried for a good hour, while they explained the impact the other's actions had on their lives. They communicated the frustrations they felt, and each volunteered that in hindsight they would have handled it differently. One apology led to a reciprocal apology, and this allowed the negotiations to begin.

3. The Desire for Fairness

"I'm not looking to get rich. I just want what I am owed. That's only fair".
—An employee who believed he was wrongfully terminated

The employee above believed that, had he not been terminated inappropriately, he would have worked at the company for three more months, and had three months of benefits, including insurance and travel expense reimbursement. He believed that was only fair. The fact that the employer had defenses to the claim and wanted to reduce any amount paid to the employee based on a percentage risk allocation did not impress the employee. He did not care; he only wanted what was "fair." However, the legal argument of "mitigation" did resonate with him. Once he learned a court would deduct his actual earnings from his measure of damages, he thought that was "fair."

"I don't want their money. I don't want to start a new job somewhere else. I just want my promotion. I only want what I've earned. That's what's fair."
—An employee with a claim for race discrimination

In this case, the employee was the only African American at a manufacturing plant. He was an hourly employee, earning less than $50,000 a year, with overtime. He had filed several EEOC charges, including one for retaliation. The employer was willing to pay the employee hundreds of thousands of dollars, if the employee would only resign. They valued his performance but did not want to deal with continual claims and charges.

The employee told me he was only a few years away from retiring, and then he and his wife were going to start a business. The money offered him would have enabled him to start that business with a nice cushion. But he was not interested; he just believed he deserved a promotion that went to someone else. He wanted to finish out his years and leave on his terms. He realized there was no guarantee he would be retained for all those additional years, but he just wanted to work. He enjoyed his work and wanted only to continue; he had been there for 18 years.

The amount the employer offered kept increasing in the face of the employee's insistence on retaining his job. However, this was not a strategy by the employee. He kept repeating he did not want money, he did not want to get rich, he did not want hundreds of thousands of dollars that he had not "earned." His driving force was to obtain what was "fair," and no more. Ultimately, the matter resolved and he was able to negotiate the promotion.

4. The Desire To Know

This desire appears when an executive is terminated and not told the true reasons why. The executive is simply told, "Things are not working out and we want to take the company in a new direction." This is the classic "non-reason." It may be perfectly legal when the employer is not required to provide a reason. Typically, only non-exempt (protected) employees in the government setting have a due process right to notice of a reason. In the private sector, only those with a contractual or union-negotiated right to a "cause" termination may be entitled to notice. However, the problem with this approach is that there always is a reason. What is it, and why doesn't the employer want to share it?

Where reasons are not given, employees will often seek legal representation. The lawyer will look for potential illegal reasons—discrimination on the basis of sex, age, disability, or perhaps retaliation for engaging in protected activity—and will file a claim.

In one matter, the company did not want to disclose the true reasons to an executive. The reasons were essentially political, and the employer did not want to hurt the executive's feelings or ability to obtain future employment by putting the reasons on paper, and did not want to have to justify itself. Frustrated at what he perceived was an unjust termination, the executive filed a claim seeking hundreds of thousands of dollars, alleging illegal retaliation.

At the mediation, he stated that he was driven by the desire to know the real reason. For hours, the company insisted it did not need to provide one. While true, I informed the company that the employee would not resolve his claim until he was informed of the real reason. The company then chose to reveal the information. Once that occurred, the executive realized that although he could argue against the action, attempting to do so would most likely be futile. He then realized it would be to his advantage to avoid negative publicity, and the case resolved.

In another matter, the employee pursued a claim for discrimination because the employer refused to disclose whether it had taken any disciplinary action against a manager who had sexually harassed the employee. The company refused to do so based on counsel's advice that there was no "need to know" and the harasser had privacy rights as well. Frustrated, the employee turned to her own lawyer to pursue a claim for discrimination.

For hours during the mediation, the employer refused to disclose what action it had taken. Ultimately, the employer agreed to disclose the information, and the employee learned that extremely serious action had been taken—the company had terminated the harasser. Unfortunately, the employee had quit work after the alleged harassment. She had a claim for lost wages for six months that could have been completely avoided had she learned the manager was gone, as she could have returned to work. Once her need to know was satisfied, the case quickly resolved.

5. The Desire for Dignity

An executive or employee who is fired suffers a deep blow to his or her self-esteem. This is especially true when an employee is summarily fired and escorted off the property, allowed to come back to retrieve personal items only after hours. This occurs even where the employee has not done anything terribly wrong; the company decides that it is simply better to remove the employee from the premises immediately.

I have known many employees who were truly humiliated by the proce-dures employed in connection with their termination. One employee told me, "I curled up in a ball and cried for days. It was weeks before I could get out of bed. I have never had anything like that happen to me before. It was truly awful! I had to see a counselor and take medication for my anxiety and depression."

Where the employee has not found comparable employment, there is a need to restore the person's dignity so the emotional scars can heal and the person can move forward. In that case, changing the termination to a resignation, deeming the employee "eligible for rehire," and drafting a favorable letter of recommen-dation provided the dignity the employee needed.

> "What about the sixteen years I put in with the company? Doesn't that count for anything?"
> —A terminated manager whose productivity decreased

Once it was realized that the underlying desire was for departure with dignity, the company shifted its negotiating posture from one based on an analysis of liability and damages, to one based on a severance-type model. This case resolved for one week of salary for each year of service.

6. The Desire for Justice

Put another way, the desire for justice (closely related to a desire for revenge) is the desire for equal suffering—one party wants the other to hurt, so they can suffer as the other one did. Sometimes this is sought through punishment—a large settlement, verdict, or "punitive damages." Other times, it is sought through negative publicity.

In one case, the employer was about to settle two employees' claims for $1.1 million. The employees did not want to agree to confidentiality of the settlement—"We're going public with this!" They wanted to contact *60 Minutes* and publish a book about their lawsuit and the ultimate result.

This issue was discussed in mediation for many hours. The employees wanted to punish the company for its actions. However, the employer was not about to pay $1 million in settlement and endure negative publicity, so confidentiality was a critical part of the deal. The employees then had to choose—go public to satisfy the desire for justice, or obtain financial compensation for their perceived unjust treatment. Ultimately, they chose the settlement, but it was a true struggle for them.

Most people don't realize that "justice" can often be long in coming and, at best, ephemeral. First, "justice" can take years to accomplish. And a big win at trial doesn't equal justice—it brings only the certainty of appeal. The appeal process adds years to the process, as well. In addition, attorneys' fees can eat up a significant part of the proceeds, the judgment may well be subject to taxation, and when all is said and done, the huge verdict can mean simply a new settlement opportunity. And depending on the size of the company, a large verdict may just be another cost of doing business, and easily absorbed.

Finally, negative publicity can certainly hurt an organization. However, bad PR only lasts so long, and public perceptions soften over time.

Recognizing this need and bringing it to light may be important to determining whether this outcome would in fact happen, and whether it truly will bring "justice."

7. The Desire for a Realistic Result

When a party demands millions of dollars, or amounts that bear no resemblance to likely damages, the case will not settle. The same is true if the employer offers what appears to be a ridiculously low offer. I often hear, "If you can just get this into a realistic range…." "We need a mediator involved because the plaintiff just doesn't understand why his demand is ridiculous!" Or, sometimes the lawyer will call me ahead of time and say, "Look, my client has a good case, but I can't get him into a realistic range. I need your help."

Regardless of the company's evaluation of the case, when the demand far exceeds even the worst-case damages the company might face, resolution is not possible. And most people recognize that the resolution through mediation and settlement often requires some form of compromise—so a demand for the full risk a company might face won't help move the process along, either. Similarly, offers of zero or nominal amounts won't help. The Driving Force here is to get the parties to recognize some risk and get them into a realistic range, even if it appears too high or too low to the parties. Once the demand gets into that range, the case almost always will settle.

8. The Desire To Do Better Than Expected

Counsel and business executives who appear at mediation are often given certain "authority" ahead of the mediation. Often they learn new information that causes them to make phone calls and see if they can obtain additional authority to pay more money. The mediator is not always told the true extent of authority. The parties' willingness to move often turns on whether they can come in lower than expected. If that's the case, they look good; they are perceived as good negotiators and congratulated on the result. This Desire can be so strong that the parties will say, "That's our top dollar," even when it's not.

"We came in less than we planned. I'm declaring victory!!"
—An e-mail sent by in-house counsel to internal executives

9. The Desire To Be Done

"This litigation has taken such a toll on me. I can't believe it has taken so long. I am so tired of having to focus on this, and meeting with our attorney, reviewing legal documents and other papers. We just want to focus on business and not have this hanging over our head!"

—A party suing on a breach of a covenant not to compete

Fortunately, the other side had the same strong feeling, and it was this driving force that ultimately brought the parties to resolution.

The desire to be done (or, the desire to stop the bleeding) shows up in two situations: The claim or litigation process has taken too much out of the parties emotionally, and/or financially. The true stress and strain of litigation were not realized until it seemed the parties were too far along to exit. From one or both parties' perspective, costs can escalate far more quickly than anticipated, and more than can be easily accommodated.

In one case, an employer spent more than $25,000 in legal fees for discovery matters in arbitration, and still, the employee had managed to provide essentially no information. Arbitration is supposed to be quicker and more economical than litigation, but in this case, a year and a half had passed and the parties had made virtually no progress in pushing the case forward. The employer was extremely frustrated and sought mediation to stop the bleeding—only to stop the endless flow of money.

In another matter, a party spent $700,000 in defense costs over three years and was anticipating a loss at trial. Counsel's primary directive, ultimately achieved, was to "get it settled," cap the loss, and stop the bleeding.

Closing Thoughts

1. Though a demand may be made in terms of money, the desire for money or financial security is not always the strongest motivator.
2. The underlying desires to be heard, to regain one's dignity, to know the "truth," to hear an apology, to achieve justice or revenge, or just to be done, may be the true motivators.
3. People are often not fully aware of their true motivations until they start speaking.
4. It is critically important for the mediator to encourage each person to share their perspective fully, and to emphasize that mediation allows for all aspects of one's views to be considered—legal, financial, emotional, practical, and so forth.
5. The true driving force must be addressed for resolution to occur.

CHAPTER 7

Get Through It: Emotional Stages of Mediation

Most people are apprehensive about what it going to happen when they face the other people in a room who have caused them so much pain. An important role of the mediator is to put everyone at ease. For that to happen, *you* as the mediator need to be fully at ease yourself.

Before you can even begin to work with parties to delve into the substance of conflict—what's at issue—or to deal with their actual feelings of anger, betrayal, resentment, etc., you need to be fully aware of the emotional stages most people experience during a mediation.

Going through mediation is an emotional experience that often brings to the surface pent-up feelings aroused by the conflict in the workplace. Indeed, I often think that the emotions expressed in mediation can be measured by the number of Kleenex the parties ask for during the process. (I keep a large supply handy.)

In my practice, I have observed many different kinds of emotions in both parties, but particularly in the employee. Sometimes it is fear of seeing the person whose actions led to the mediation ("You mean I have to see my boss at the joint session? He's the one who did this to me!"), anger because that person is not at the joint session ("The company didn't even bring my boss—and he was the main person involved in all this!"), and frustration ("Why don't they just pay us what we ask?").

It's vitally important for mediators and conflict-solvers to understand the emotional aspects of mediation, when they tend to find expression during the process, and how these emotions can help lead to resolution.

When temporary pessimism strikes, the mediator can provide needed reassurance that progress is, in fact, being made.

Armed with this knowledge, you will be mindful of the structure, so that you can know that progress is being made. Keep your eye on the ball, so you can assist everyone in moving through the different emotional stages of the mediation process.

The A-List of Emotions in Mediation

Anxiety. Anxiety is the most common emotion experienced by parties waiting for mediation to begin. They have been on an emotional rollercoaster dealing with their conflict for quite some time. They know their own views of the conflict and strongly believe in the rightness of their positions. They each believe the other is being unreasonable. They fear that the conflict will escalate, so that the goal of resolving the dispute in mediation will not be achieved.

You can easily tell anxiety is present from the parties' body language (such as clenched hands, arms held across the abdomen, or hunched carriage) and facial expressions. If attorneys are present, they may be laughing and sharing pleasantries with each other. They may even be sitting in a forward-leaning position, expressing that they are "ready to go." However, the parties are usually leaning back, waiting tensely for the session to begin. They may not even be speaking.

Anger. Anger often goes hand in hand with disputes. If a person believes his position is right, the other side must be wrong and is being unreasonable in failing to agree to his demands. While a conflict remains unresolved, he can become obsessed and relive it over and over, thereby increasing the stress and the anger he feels feel toward his adversary.

Negative feelings like anger can cause people to become less productive professionally and greatly harm personal relationships.

A person in conflict may know intellectually that displaying anger is unlikely to help him achieve a resolution, yet, be unable to prevent an angry outburst or other negative expression that could derail the mediation.

Adrenaline. When people argue their positions, beliefs, and feelings to those who disagree with them, they expend a significant amount of emotional energy asserting the righteousness of their position. As a result, their bodies are likely to produce adrenaline. This hormone is produced by the adrenal glands when the body is in a state of high anxiety, fear, or excitement. In a sense it enhances alertness and prepares the body for battle or fleeing. This is the "fight or flight" reaction people typically have when in conflict.

Awareness. Before mediation begins, the parties usually know their respective positions—but not what led to those positions or the underlying interests or needs of the other side. This is especially true where there is a breakdown in communications between the involved individuals, who then get lawyers involved. Even when there has been communication, the parties may have been unable or unwilling to really listen to what the other had to say.

I have yet to mediate a dispute in which the parties did not learn something they did not know before they came to the mediation. The "something" could be a document, a statement someone made or heard, or an e-mail someone sent. It could be how someone felt about something that happened, or a legal argument not previously thought of, or a fact not previously considered. Perhaps the employee never complained to the company's human resources department before filing suit, or never consulted with the ombudsperson.

Typically, this new awareness leads to the "magic" of mediation. The magic is the willingness of parties, based on new information, to view the conflict in a different light. It is this willingness that opens the door to resolution.

Mediation often provides the first opportunity people have to become fully aware of what each other's views are.

Acknowledgment. When new information comes to light in mediation and the mediator communicates it to the other party, what usually follows is a verbal acknowledgment that this information was not previously considered. One employee confessed during the caucus, "I never realized I could have gone to Human Resources. Perhaps I should have before I quit. I do see things a bit differently now; I might even lose this case because I quit before complaining."

Analysis. The acknowledgment of new information typically leads to a new analysis of the disputed issues that takes this information into account. Each new fact can affect the dynamics in mediation. Thus, the parties cannot stand pat on their positions. For example, an employer may learn during the mediation that the employee would make a great witness and decide that this information warrants a change in its position. This happened in one mediation where the employer's human resources manager told me in a private session, "We had no idea she would come across so well. We'll increase our offer because the jury is going to love her."

The result is a willingness to shift closer towards an amicable resolution. Even a slight shift can start the ball rolling.

Active Participation. Progress often fosters progress. So when one side makes an accommodation by changing its position, the other side is more likely to reciprocate. In this way, the parties begin to actively participate in the give and take of mediation. They see that the process requires moving away from hardened positions toward reaching an agreement that is acceptable to both sides. This creates an environment in which they can reach a mutually acceptable settlement.

Acceptance. When parties finally reach the point where they feel accepting of an outcome, the final resolution rarely looks exactly like either side envisioned it would before the mediation, since it could contain items or terms that they initially believed were not appropriate.

Closing Thoughts

1. Mediation Success focuses on the process, the substance and the emotion of conflict.
2. The mediator is attuned to the true underlying interests, while remaining ever-mindful of the process and the emotional stages.

3. The mediator can tell where the parties are in the process, takes steps to ensure forward progress is being made.
4. When temporary pessimism strikes, the mediator can provide needed reassurance that progress is, in fact, being made. This reassurance instills hope and provides optimism.

CHAPTER 8

Get it Over:
Embrace the Emotion

Just before a mediation was about to begin, a lawyer asked if he could speak with me privately for a moment. We stepped into an office, and he confided, "I wanted to let you know, I'm having a problem with my client. He's really emotional about this. I have done my best. I told him we needed to keep the emotion out of it, but I'm afraid my words have had no effect. I thought you should be prepared."

The lawyer was clearly concerned, because he feared that his client's emotion would get the best of him and escalate tension. It might even derail the mediation.

"No worries," I said. "That's perfectly okay. It's normal to feel stressed in this situation, and I'm used to dealing with strong emotions in this context. You're the lawyer, and it's your job to deal with the legal aspects of the case. I'm the mediator, and you can trust me to handle the emotional aspects of resolution."

I gave him a smile of encouragement, and we began the mediation. When it came time to get it out, I made sure to give his client enough time to tell not only his perspective, but also to go on at some length about how upset he was, how wrong he thought the other party was, and how much the whole lawsuit had impacted his life. The lawyer gratefully sat back and let it unfold. His client's venting took about an hour.

Not surprisingly, after the client was done, the client said, "Wow, man, that felt good to tell someone exactly what I've been feeling!"

The mediation proceeded and we resolved the case later in the day.

Armed with the knowledge that the expression of strong emotion is expected, normal, and actually helpful to mediation, you can then use this knowledge to support mediation success.

Achieve Mediation Success by establishing, and guiding, the process so that emotions are not barriers, but instead are used as positive tools for resolution.

Don't *Suppress* Yourself. *Express* Yourself.

The fact is, when you repress strong emotion, you do not do yourself any favors. This is true for several reasons.

First, the other people to the conflict likely do not know the true depth about what you are feeling, and why you might be feeling that way. Many times, what someone is truly angry about is not what the other side thought.

For example, one side might be mad because they were never given an apology; they were never told the reason for the other side's decisions; or they were never given an opportunity to address a complaint.

They may be less distraught about the fact that they haven't worked in some time, than the fact that the lawsuit has been so expensive and time-consuming.

In one case I was involved with, one person literally could not begin to address the substance of the dispute until he got an explanation as to why the other side just didn't pick up the phone and call him to resolve it. That question was keeping him up at night. Although the other side felt it was irrelevant, this was a major cause of anger and frustration, which had to be revealed, and addressed, in order to allow progress to be made in the mediation.

It is only when the true depth and causes of emotion are known that attention can be focused on addressing the reasons, with the goal of reducing the negative tension.

The mediator or conflict-solver can rephrase the expression of emotion in a non-confrontational way to the other side, to increase understanding of the root cause. It may be that the emotion or anger is based on a belief about something that is not accurate, or on an assumption that is not true.

Some people are taught from an early age not to display emotion. Others may have been told not to show emotion in front of the other party, or even to "stick to the facts." Suppression of honest emotion is often what brings parties to conflict.

Yet, for more than a century, therapists have been aware of the psychological harm done by the repression of emotion. It is like a physical weight that can, in some cases, cause physical harm from the stress of keeping it in.

As far back as the early 1900s, psychologists have recognized the healing benefits that occur when we are allowed to vent freely about traumatic events and related true expression of emotions. This has been referred to by Dr. Joseph Breuer and others as the "catharsis theory" which serves as the fundamental basis of psychoanalysis. In fact, Dr. Sigmund Freud has been said to have referred to psychoanalysis as the "talking cure."

The fact is that when we talk about what's bothering us, and how angry we are, we feel better. Think about common descriptors in this situation. We "let off steam." It's like the teapot about to boil over—the steam keeps it from doing so. We "get it off our chest," referring to lifting the burden.

Only when the emotion has been released, can we begin to heal—to "get it over."

Mediation Success Rule #10:
Go to the emotion, not away from it.

It follows from the above, that one of the essential keys to mediation success is this: *embrace* the emotion. Welcome the expression of anger, frustration, and pain. This is an expression of the internal conflict felt by a party to a strong conflict. The release benefits the speaker, and helps to clear their mind and body.

One client said, at the start of a mediation, "I feel really nervous, sort of like when I was in high school, going to a dance, looking across the gym floor and dreading asking a girl to dance!"

I smiled at the analogy, and offered assurance that he won't be rejected. I told him I would do my best to make the process as painless as possible. I appreciated his candor. I offered, "No worries—I'll dance with you!"

It was a wonderful ice-breaker that set the tone for open communication during the mediation.

Open venting is critical to allow one to move on to the resolution phase of the mediation. The mediator or conflict-resolver should provide support by telling the party that it is natural to feel such strong emotions, and by expressly stating that he or she is "going to do all I can to help get this resolved, and get you to a better place, so you can move on."

Internal vs. External Conflict

In any given conflict situation, there are often two distinct conflicts: the external conflict, which is the one they are in the courtroom or the conference room for; and the internal conflict, the feelings and emotions with which he or she has been wrestling.

In addition to the anger or frustration felt towards the other side, it's not unusual for one to be somewhat angry or frustrated with themselves. This is one form of internal conflict.

They might feel that they have let the situation get to them, and they wished they did not.

They may feel a strong need to repress because they do not want to escalate or derail the situation, or because they want to remain "calm, cool, and collected."

They might be volatile in their presentation because they are expending huge amounts of emotional energy in seeking acknowledgement, understanding, and validation to justify to themselves that it is reasonable and appropriate for them to feel as strongly as they do.

The mediator's job includes recognizing and accepting the internal conflict that is occurring when there is a strong display of emotion. The internal struggle must be revealed, and the person's concerns and feelings addressed with acceptance and empathy.

Catharsis and non-judgmental acceptance and support are essential steps to allowing the parties to address the external conflict: the dispute with the other party.

Before the external conflict with the other party can be addressed and resolved, the internal conflict has to be addressed and dissipated, enough so that the person's mind feels calm enough to be able to absorb the information and appropriately participate in the give-and-take of the negotiation and mediation process.

By receiving support in the form of validation of the fact that such strong feelings are normal and acceptable, the internal conflict is addressed and de-escalated.

So how can the mediator or conflict-resolver go to the emotion, and not away from it? By knowing—and conveying—the following four essential truths.

Truth #1: Tears are Good

If I had to estimate, I'd say that in half of the mediations I've handled, whether in the workplace or in a court case, tears are involved.

Why are they crying? Are they in deep pain? What do the tears signify?

Tears are the strongest non-verbal communicator that exists. Let them come, and listen for what lies underneath.

Gratitude and Relief

Ever notice that when you are in deep pain, and someone is kind to you, your eyes well up? Why is that?

Tears come because we are nervous, anxious, tense, and in pain. We are struggling internally with our feelings, worrying that we will not be able to restrain ourselves from becoming emotional, and worrying further that we will be judged negatively if we do, because other people will not understand.

When someone displays empathy, it is often unexpected, and a huge relief. We are so grateful that someone has understood the depth of our emotion, and has not judged us harshly. The empathy is a gift. It is our gratitude for true kindness that often moves us to tears.

This is a positive and necessary step in conflict resolution. When we no longer have to pour psychic energy into our internal conflict, in an effort to bury our feelings, we free up our mental abilities to address and resolve the problem at hand.

Despair and Depression

Tears can also signify deep despair and depression. Listen to what one man said in a recent mediation.

"I cry all the time. I loved this place. I worked here for almost my entire adult life! I won awards for customer service. I need to tell you, when they told me I was being investigated for violation of a work policy, I cried. They suspended me, and I cried. They terminated me, and I cried.

"They eventually reinstated me after 10 months, and an arbitrator decided that I should not have been fired—but the whole thing was terrible! They only did this because I am African American, I know. I shouldn't be here! They shouldn't have treated me this way!

I'm still crying and I can't stop. I'm on Prozac and Xanax, but nothing works. I'm still crying!"

This man was deeply embarrassed, both by the fact that he had been accused of wrongdoing, and by the display of his own strong emotion he was unable to control.

This man was in deep despair of ever being able to regain some quality of life. After so much time, he knew he should have been able to move on—but he was not able to.

He said, "I survived family tragedies including the death of my parents. I got over that. This is just a job, I know, but I can't get past what they did to me!"

I told him I understood the strength of what he was feeling, and that it was normal for someone who feels he has been unjustly accused and pushed out of his job—especially one he has given his life to—to become deeply depressed.

I told him his tears were good, and that it was okay to cry.

I also asked him what he wanted for his future. Did he want to continue working at this job, or did he want a resolution that would allow him to close this chapter and move on with his life, perhaps in a new job?

With tears flowing, he said that if there was a way that we could structure a resolution to enable him to retire, that was what his doctor and his friends and family thought would be best. This was the result we ultimately achieved, so that he could move on and get back to the business of living.

After the settlement documents were signed, I reached out to shake the employee's hand. He stood up from his chair, and hugged me—tight. "Thank you, thank you so much!" he said. "I can't tell you how glad I am about this outcome."

Embarrassment and Fear

When a claim is filed by a current, as opposed to a former, employee, tears typically suggest not only embarrassment and humiliation, but deep concern and fear about what the future holds.

An employee in deep conflict needs to know what options are available to him. Are the parties working toward a resolution that keeps him working at the company, or one that contemplates departure?

Most employers, when faced with a monetary demand for resolution by a current employee who has filed a lawsuit, are reluctant to put any sort of serious money towards a resolution if the employee remains employed.

This is because others in the workplace will likely hear about the settlement, and also because the potential exists, if the employee is later disciplined, he or she will claim "retaliation" and file another lawsuit. If the employer can ensure this will not occur by reaching a resolution where the employee leaves the company, that employer is likely to be far more generous in the negotiations.

In one case, an executive was so upset about the way he had been treated by his supervisor that he impulsively quit. He regretted his action, but it was too late—the employer accepted his resignation. He filed for unemployment and the employer fought that, too. He was humiliated and filed a claim with the EEOC claiming the company discriminated against him based on age.

In the mediation, he vowed to fight until the end. His wife, though, pleaded with him to consider an outcome that allowed him to move past the strain and stress of his situation. She was afraid that, if the conflict continued, it would spell the end of his peace and sense of self.

A settlement was reached that included a letter of reference, and an amount of money that enabled him to depart with dignity. At the end of the mediation, both he and his wife were grateful to be able to put the matter behind them and move on.

Truth #2: Anger is Natural

Who wouldn't be angry if they were being called on the carpet, in danger of losing their job because of another employee's complaint?

Who wouldn't be angry if they had been unjustly fired and were now humiliated, embarrassed, and financially insecure?

Who wouldn't be angry if they were sued and forced to pay huge legal bills?

No one is ever happy about whatever caused them to be in serious conflict, or about the fact that they are now caused to suffer through litigation. Frankly, people in general are not even happy to take a day out of their lives for mediation.

It's not unusual for a person to say after a mediation, "Well, I'm glad it's over. It was good to meet you. No offense, but I hope I don't have to see you again!"

A true gift that the mediator can give a party is permission to be angry. This permission is unexpected, and freeing. This permission amazingly often has the paradoxical effect of dissipating the anger.

This works to de-escalate conflict. The reason is easily understood. When we expend valuable emotional resources convincing those present that we are angry and our anger is justified, we are focused on that task. It serves to block our ability to get to the next step: problem-solving.

So, let someone who is upset or angry express that anger. This way, they will be able to re-direct their valuable energy instead to creatively focusing on options for resolution.

Displaying anger at a joint session is acceptable, unless it escalates to such a point where it may block resolution absent intervention. At that point, it is best to address the anger in a separate meeting.

Consider the case I call, "The Angry Lawyer." I mediated a business dispute where the lawyer was representing himself. He had apparently been through a divorce and had lost his house due to economic factors. The client on the opposite side was represented by an independent lawyer.

In just the first few minutes of the opening session, where I was covering the process of mediation and the exchange of information, apparently the lawyer who was representing himself said a profanity under his breath to the other lawyer.

I did not hear anything, as I had been writing a note on a legal pad at the time. The opposing lawyer said, "Did you hear that? Did you hear that? He just told me to f*** off!"

"I did not!" exclaimed the other lawyer.

"You did too!"

"No, I didn't. I told you to shut the f*** up."

Here was my first thought:

"Really? These are grown men, lawyers who are supposed to be professional. My time is valuable as well, and I don't need to spend my time with people like this. I'm sure I have better things to do, and I should just send these guys packing."

Then, I had my mediator-considered thought: "Okay, that's why we are here. They have not proven capable of getting past the anger to resolution. Just address what's going on and get past this."

You know the old legal proverb, "A lawyer who is representing himself has a fool for a client." This lawyer who was representing himself clearly needed some assistance.

I looked at each of them, and said, "Okay, stop. Please. Both of you. Time to move into separate session." I escorted one group out.

The second lawyer immediately apologized to me. "I'm so sorry, I owe you an apology. I just let him get to me! That's never happened to me before."

I acknowledged his apology. "All is well, no worries. Let me speak to him and I'll get this done."

I returned to the room with the lawyer who was representing himself. With him was his paralegal and a law clerk who were giving both his aggressive display of anger and his legal position full support. I asked if I could speak with him privately.

"I can see you are extremely angry. I know you're upset, things have not gone well for you, and you are not happy about being here."

"Yes, that is definitely true," he said.

"Do you want to get this done?" I asked.

"Yes! I do! I'm sorry about what happened."

"Okay. It's done. Let's move past it and focus on resolution, shall we? Will you let me help you?"

"Yes, of course."

"And, no more profanity, okay?"

"Okay, okay, absolutely. Again, I'm sorry. That shouldn't have happened," he said.

We got past it, and got it resolved.

The learning point here is this: It's okay to be angry. It's a natural component of conflict and the frustration that comes with the adversarial nature of the legal system, or with the fact that another will not act in a way that you believe is reasonable.

As a general rule, it is best to meet anger with calmness and a firm approach, not with equal anger. If you model a calm response, since behavior is reciprocal, it will tend to bring the other party's intense feeling to a lower, more reasonable level where critical thinking can be brought into play.

Behavior is reciprocal, so it is best to meet anger with calmness and a firm approach.

Expressing anger is acceptable and it can often be a necessary release. There is no reason to be intimidated by anger.

In over a thousand mediations, anger has been expressed more times than I can count. I have yet to have a matter not resolve due to a display of anger. That is because I accept it as natural, and allow it—to the limited extent needed to allow the person to vent and explain what it's about for them.

Once anger has been displayed, and people are reminded of the goal of reaching resolution—their reason for being present—they almost always apologize for the intensity of their outburst and proceed in a much calmer fashion.

Truth #3: Touch is Powerful

Touching is not necessary. It may well be inappropriate and an invasion of another's space to reach out and hug someone you just met that is in tears or is clearly in deep pain. In some cultures, personal touch is taboo.

Yet, in some instances, even the smallest touch or gesture can have a huge effect.

There have been occasions over the years in mediation when I have simply leaned forward and gently placed a hand on top of the hand of a person in tears, or on top of their arm if it is resting on the table, for a brief moment. This small gesture, accompanied by the words "I understand," or "It's okay, take your time," brings immense comfort.

Here are two stories that illustrate the point.

The Terminated CEO and the Empathic Touch

The Chair of the Board of Directors called the CEO and requested her presence at a meeting with the Board's Executive Committee. At the meeting, the CEO was placed on leave and shortly thereafter terminated.

The CEO later learned that her termination was due to a survey that had been taken of a number of employees, without her knowledge. She was told that she was perceived to be disrespectful, abusive, and intimidating; that her negative behavior had caused valued staff members to leave. The details of the survey were not shared with her. Rather, she was told, "Your leadership is no longer consistent with our mission."

The CEO was angry that she was not given the ability to rebut or otherwise address any of the complaints in the survey. She was humiliated and offended by the way the Board handled the situation. And, she was deeply concerned about the impact on her reputation, which she had worked 35 years to build.

The CEO retained counsel, and wrote a letter indicating her intent to sue the company for defamation. The company agreed to mediate.

The CEO was highly educated and articulate, and spoke about the circumstances without displaying much emotion. Yet, the effort she was expending in reigning in her feelings was plain on her face. The tension was evident in her posture.

I moved from my seat at the end of the conference table, to a seat next to her. I reached out and touched her hand.

The gesture moved her to tears.

She expressed that it was the first time in her life she had ever shed a tear over work, and said that she was embarrassed at what she perceived was an unprofessional reaction on her part. Yet, this was a watershed moment for her, and the case resolved shortly thereafter.

The small connection said, "I care. It's okay to cry. I am here to see about bringing you peace and respect."

This gift of acceptance, empathy, and caring allowed the tears to come and removed the wall of internal conflict, which had previously stood as a barrier to resolution.

A severance package was negotiated, which, in addition to financial components, contained a mutual non-disparagement provision, a resignation letter from the CEO, and a mutually agreed-upon memo to be sent to staff explaining the CEO's departure.

Her dignity was preserved, and the reputation of both the executive and the company was spared from unnecessary media speculation.

"At least now I can hold my head high and move on," she said at the end of the day.

The Bully and The Assertive Touch

On other occasions, touching someone's arm in an affirmative way can be a needed, assertive method of conveying to someone that they should seriously consider what you have to say.

In one mediation, the lawyers confided in me the day before that their client was a somewhat of a bully, one with whom even they had difficulty dealing. They were not sure if he always was truthful. They stressed to me privately that there were serious problems with the case and that they really needed to get it settled.

As predicted, the client was stubborn and reluctant to negotiate seriously. The company was being sued in a class action by numerous former employees. After six hours in mediation, he packed up his briefcase and snapped it shut, and stood up to leave. He had yet to make a serious offer on the case.

His lawyers were frustrated, but felt their hands were tied. They looked at me with a look that said, "Hey—we're stuck. What can you *do* here??"

I asked their permission to speak with their client privately, which they gave me.

We stepped outside. The client was a very tall man, perhaps 6'5". I am relatively short. He immediately began complaining about the huge amount he'd paid in legal bills. He was so caught up in his ranting and raving about the injustice of the lawsuit and his bills, that he was not focusing on how he could stop the pain.

I placed both my hands on his forearms. "Listen to me," I said. "I apologize for touching you this way, but I need you to listen to me. Do you want to resolve this?"

"Yes!" he said emphatically.

"Well, okay then. Put $100,000.00 on the table. They won't take it, but it will be a start. I promise you I will stay with it. You don't have to do as I suggest. But if you want to settle this, this is what it is going to take to get it going."

I do not advocate as a general rule invading someone's space by touching them. However, it's important to judge what interventions might be called for to help the party overcome his own actions that will hurt their ability to resolve the dispute. They come to you because the parties themselves have been unable through logical discussion to reach a resolution.

Assistance is needed in whatever form it takes to get the deal done and reach resolution. If you have been successful in establishing rapport early on in the mediation, that rapport will allow a party to be receptive to your efforts. A touch can be far more effective than verbally trying to rationalize with someone who is deeply angry or upset.

In this case, the client took some time to absorb this, met with his own lawyers for a few minutes, and made the offer. Although the matter did not resolve that day, the other side now had hope that real money was in play and they were willing to continue negotiations.

After some weeks of follow up, the matter resolved.

Truth #4: Empathy Is Better Than Sympathy

Although sympathy is nice, most of us really don't want others to feel sorry for us or to pity us. What we truly want is empathy. We want to know someone else has been there, and that she understands our pain.

Just as important, we want to know another person has been where we are, faced the same or similar demons, and *survived*. It is especially helpful to know that they not only slayed the monster, but emerged stronger and better than before.

Of course, empathy can always be expressed by the simple statement, "I understand." But the best and most effective way to show empathy is to share a story about a time when you, or a friend, colleague, or family member experienced something similar, and conquered it. This kind of empathy provides encouragement and hope—essential keys to mediation success.

Share Your Own Story

I was mediating a claim for sexual harassment against an employer. The employee was Muslim, and did not speak English very well. We worked with an interpreter.

The employee did not have any lost wages, because she had not left her job, but she felt deeply harmed by the repeated offensive comments and physical advances made on her by one of the managers at work. She did not think anyone understood how badly it upset her. It caused her to lose sleep and be afraid to go to work everyday, and impacted her marriage.

Finally, she went to the EEOC, and filed a charge. As a result, the employer took the complaint seriously, conducted an investigation, and the conduct stopped. Months later, though, she was still extremely distressed about the circumstances.

During the first hour or so that we spent together, I was not sure if I was making much progress. She seemed pretty fixed on a specific resolution that she wanted, in terms of a dollar amount. She kept repeating, "You do not understand. No one can understand."

The employer eventually offered her the amount of money she had asked for. Still, she did not want to accept the offer. She was still upset.

I asked to meet with her privately. I then shared with her a story about when I was a young lawyer, working in a law firm. I told her about sexual harassment I experienced from one of the partners, how I reacted to it, and how it made me feel; how I'd gone to a lawyer, and how, ultimately, I chose to leave the law firm.

My story brought tears to her eyes. She nodded. She now knew that I understood. We connected.

That connection opened the door to resolution, and we resolved the matter.

As she was leaving, she reached out and hugged me, and said, "Thank you. Thank you for telling me your story."

It made all the difference to her. She knew she was not alone, and she saw how I could now tell the story of something that happened a long time ago, that I moved past and went on to have a successful career and a good life.

"I, Too, Have Been Sued."

I've had occasion to share in mediation that I was once sued. A car dealer took a new car back in trade from me that I had bought just a few days before in another state. I had driven it home and realized it was the wrong car for me, for a variety of reasons, including a mechanical issue.

The dealer in my home state had reassured me that although I was losing several thousand dollars, I would not have to pay to register the car and would save about two thousand dollars, which would help. I would not have bought the car without that reassurance.

Some months later, apparently the dealership was made to pay the registration fee and served my husband and I with a lawsuit. I was convinced we were right—but still, the notion that I had been sued was awful. It caused me angst right up until the day of the hearing in Small Claims Court.

My husband and I had to take the morning off of work to prepare for and attend the hearing. My heart was literally pounding as I walked through the courthouse.

The judge ruled in our favor, but still, we weren't certain that he would. The whole thing was an unpleasant experience I would not want to repeat. And that was a relatively minor matter.

"I, Too, Have Brought a Claim."

In another situation, I brought suit against someone who owed me money. I offered to resolve it for less, but for two years he would not discuss resolution.

We were forced to file suit, and ended up with the matter set for an arbitration. (The amount was under $50,000 so it was subject to mandatory arbitration.) We arrived at the location for the hearing. We sat in the conference room, making small talk with the opposing counsel and his witness.

My hands were clammy and I was nervous. Where the heck was the arbitrator?

It turned out the arbitrator had not calendared the hearing and so would not be appearing. Faced with rescheduling, my attorney asked the other party if he was interested in discussing settlement now. Finally, he was.

I ended up resolving the matter for about half of what I was owed. Although my lawyer said I was clearly owed the money, as a black-and-white matter of contract law, frankly after two years I was just happy to have it behind me.

Even though I had brought the suit, it weighed on me for the better part of two years. I never dreamed that I myself would need to retain counsel and would end up in a legal dispute. I was just glad to be done. I learned a valuable business lesson in the process regarding collection of payment.

I received the settlement check. I promptly deposited the check in the bank, but I took a portion of the proceeds directly to a local jewelry store, where I purchased a lovely piece of jewelry I'd been looking at longingly for some time.

Even though we had some taxes due and could have used the money for a better purpose, the ring I bought made me happy. So, I got something out of the dispute after all.

The above stories are true, and taught me empathy with someone who has been sued, and someone who has filed suit. I learned first-hand about the fact that the length of time it takes to process the case, and the toll it can take, is often unexpected.

I have told the story about the ring (that's the way I think of it) many times in mediation. It never fails to bring a smile to the faces of those I am working with who have filed a suit and are considering whether to accept less than what they came in wanting.

The moral of the story is this: "It is permissible to consider accepting less. There are added benefits, including both being done with the tension from this process and using the money for other things."

It is only when the emotional component has been adequately cared for, that most people can move to a focus on the real reason they are in mediation, which is to explore ways to resolve the dispute.

Closing Thoughts

1. To help others get it over, accept and embrace strong emotion.
2. Recognize there are often two distinct conflicts: the internal one and the external one.
3. Tears are good. Let the tears come, and seek to understand what they signify about the internal conflict.
4. Anger is natural. Acknowledge the legitimacy and accept the expression of anger—it will free up valuable energy for problem-solving once the anger has been expressed.
5. Touch is powerful. If appropriate, reach out and touch. Use your non-verbal skills to convey a strong message of empathy or to draw attention to the need to consider a different angle.
6. Empathy is better than sympathy. Share your own stories. Remember we all want to be understood, and to believe we can survive and move past the current situation to get back to the business of life.

PART FOUR:

The Resolution

CHAPTER 9

Get the Money Right:
The Drama of Dollars

Of course, conflicts that are raised in the form of lawsuits or legal claims involve money. So, demands are made in terms of dollars.

As you have seen in earlier chapters, conflict is not always about the money. Even where a conflict seems to be solely about money, here are some ways to help shift the focus away from just dollars, to a focus on what that money symbolizes, and beyond that, what that money can buy to heal past hurt, and enable someone to move on.

When searching for possible ways to resolve workplace conflict, think about the symbolism of money. Understanding the drama and symbolism of dollars allows you to be open to finding creative ways to structure a solution to meet the needs of everyone involved.

The Symbolism of Money

The following eleven examples signify what can be accomplished by looking at the psychological (non-monetary) impact that offering money for certain specified reasons can have on one's state of mind. This helps meet underlying interests and enables people to overcome psychological barriers to resolution.

These psychological barriers exist for both employers and employees. The symbolism of offers can help everyone become more comfortable with offering or accepting solutions.

Mediation Success Rule #11:
Consider the symbolism of money.

1. One Year's Salary: Acknowledgement of Value

In a business or workplace dispute, it is amazing how often it seems that in cases involving high level executives, or cases where the employee is has a significant likelihood of prevailing in court, the negotiated resolution is one year's salary, or one year's salary plus attorney's fees.

No real surprise, if you think about the significance of what that payment symbolizes. Highly valued executives often are able to negotiate contracts up front which contain a provision for a one-year severance, if the executive is let go for any reason at all.

For one who has not obtained such a lucrative contract in advance of his or her employment, such a payment says, "You are the equivalent of a highly-valued executive."

This can go a long way to restoring someone's dignity.

2. Months of Pay: A Bridge to Re-employment

In mediating employment disputes, my human resource colleagues have often told me that there is an unwritten "rule of thumb" (at least in a healthy economy) that for every $10,000 of salary an employee earned, it takes roughly one month of looking to find comparable employment.

So, if a company and it's employee both agree that this is a legitimate "measuring stick," the employee who earned $50,000 per year before being terminated might consider accepting five months of his salary as an element of an acceptable resolution. It represents an essential bridge to re-employment.

Other items that can support a new start include monies for outplacement assistance with a company that specializes on helping clients rebuild careers, or a letter of recommendation. That letter can help an employee become re-employed, while at the same time providing recognition of significant past contributions of value, even though the departure was not by choice.

If the employee has been terminated, changing the termination to a resignation can be critically important to helping the employee obtain future employment.

3. Amounts Per Year of Service: Acknowledgement of Past Value

An amount of X dollars for X years of service represents an acknowledgement of valuable contribution made in the past. This symbolic payment is especially important when working on a conflict with a long-term employee.

It is not unusual for a person to feel they have been unfairly terminated for one mistake, or a few recent performance issues, when they have been with a company for many years. Even when a company does not have an official "severance" policy or plan, structuring a resolution this way helps the employee feel as if he was treated similar to a person who was laid off, due to no fault of his own.

Why should a company consider doing this? Departure with dignity has value. We spend so much of our time at work that we don't want to leave a job we spent years of our life doing feeling as if we failed. And, an employee who leaves on his own terms, or at least on terms he can feel good about, will have far greater peace in his life. A resolution that offers psychological peace and dignity is likely one that can be successful, and often is not as costly as the expense and lost productive time the company will experience in responding to an ongoing legal case.

4. Compensation for Medical Bills: Acknowledgement of Emotional Harm

Almost always, an employee who brings a lawsuit against her employer will have felt emotionally drained by perceived mistreatment. The stress harms the employee emotionally and often physically.

If an employee has suffered deep anguish and emotional distress, payment of medical expenses incurred for doctors, therapists, prescriptions, and lost time from work, even though contained in a settlement agreement where the company expressly does not admit liability, still symbolizes an acknowledgement that harm was caused. This is so, because it is offered to compensate for that loss.

Payment of an additional sum, not tied to any bill or provable expense, but to general "pain and suffering" or "emotional distress" similarly symbolizes an acknowledgement that harm was caused. This part of an offer conveys an implicit wish to apologize by offering a way to make up for that harm.

5. Payment of Health Insurance Premiums: Security

At a time when medical and insurance costs can break a family, an amount of money to pay for insurance premiums, represents protection from the risk of huge medical bills that can destroy a family.

For the person who is not currently employed, and has no sure job prospects, this payment represents needed security. The cost of monthly insurance premiums to an unemployed person can be completely out of reach, especially if a family is involved. While a person may be able to monitor and control his or her own spending, we all fear the catastrophic results of unforeseen medical illness and bills.

Offering to pay monthly health insurance premiums for the length of time it might take for an employee to become re-employed meets the fundamental need of financial security on a vital aspect of life in the world today.

6. Nominal Amounts or Costs of Defense: Nuisance Value

Sometimes a claim truly appears to have no legal basis at all. Your lawyers tell you it will likely get kicked out of court. Yet, even when a company does not fear ultimate exposure, they know they will have to spend time, attention, and money defending the claim. Therefore, they might as a result, offer a nominal amount (recognizing each person's perception of nominal may vary) as a "nuisance" value settlement.

Of course, what each person perceives as "nominal" can vary greatly, from a few hundred dollars to even $25,000 or a sum in that range. Regardless of the exact amount, payment of a nominal amount of money symbolizes that the company does not take the matter seriously from a legal perspective, but sees the value in offering something to get rid of the nuisance.

Similarly, a company may offer an amount that equates to their costs of defense. For example, their lawyers may estimate that the company could pay $50,000 to have the case kicked out on legal motions.

A company's offer to pay an amount equal to what they believe they will expend on legal fees and costs indicates that they do not believe the claim has merit, but they do recognize they would have to expend that sum to win. It also is a clear way to eliminate the risk, albeit a small one, of a loss or outcome much worse than they predict.

In other words, it symbolizes what many may feel is a prudent business decision.

7. Payment of Debt: Freedom to Move On

In one case I mediated, the attorneys argued back and forth about the value of the case. The dichotomy ranged from a low of $15,000 to a high of $75,000.

Hours into the mediation, the employee told me she owed her mother $26,000, the amount she had needed to support herself since her termination.

In spite of what the lawyers felt the case was worth, the case resolved for the $26,000 amount of the employee's debt, plus her attorney's fees. To the employee, that resolution represented freedom from debt—which allowed her to move on with her life.

8. Payment of Tuition: A Fresh Start

There are times when the conflict between an employee and his company has reached such a high level, and/or has become so public in the industry in which they operate, that a person feels his options to continue in his chosen field are so limited that he feels he has to start over.

The idea of starting over can be daunting. Fortunately, I have had several cases where an employer agreed to pay for tuition at a local university. This creative solution allowed the employee to make a fresh start, with new skills and abilities.

Litigation and unresolved conflict keeps the person who believes he or she has been mistreated mired in the past. They fight because they believe this is the only choice they have: to prove that what happened to them was unfair and should be compensated.

The option of a new and different future is exciting and full of opportunity. Choosing a new career path enables a person to look at the world with different eyes, and helps them to focus on the future instead of the past.

9. Attorney's Fees: Cause of Financial Harm

Payment of an employee's attorney's fees may provide validation that the employer's actions were the cause of forced retention of counsel. It is not unusual, for that reason, for a company to refuse to pay any amount towards attorney's fees. This can symbolize to the company that the employee was reasonable in hiring counsel, and it may be hard to digest if the company feels they are being unjustly accused.

A company may also be concerned about precedent, if other employees learn about the resolution. The fear or concern is that others will jump on the bandwagon, hire lawyers and bring claims, believing the company will ultimately reimburse that cost, regardless of the merits of the claim.

Payment of some or all of attorney's fees incurred, however, may be necessary to provide needed freedom from debt, to allow the employee to move on.

Several forward-thinking companies offer mediation policies where they offer to pay a specified amount, usually in the range of $2,000, for counsel who represent employees in a company-paid mediation program. This is a smart way to allow the employee to gain needed legal advice so that he or she can be guided in making appropriate decisions about resolution, while capping potential exposure for an employee's legal fees.

10. Splitting the Difference: A Business Decision

"Splitting the difference" in monetary terms never feels good at the outset. That is because it is vitally important to allow each person to discuss the differing perspectives, to turn the facts over, to try out their strategies, and to test. Thomas Paine once said, "We value too lightly that which comes too easily."

Here's a story to illustrate this point.

I was serving as a mediator in a securities fraud case. After the joint session, we broke into separate sessions. One party was a business that consisted of three owners, who were present along with their lawyer. Their lawyer said he was going step outside for a moment. We assumed he was going to make a call.

He was gone for about 30 minutes, during which time his clients relayed to me many of the specifics about their matter. They were not quite through when their lawyer came back into the room.

"I did it!" he proudly said.

"Did what?" asked his clients.

"I settled the case!"

"What are you talking about? We are in here with the mediator. We aren't even through talking to her!"

"Well, no need to anymore. You told me at breakfast what you were willing to pay. I pulled the other lawyer out of the room, we negotiated a bit, and I settled it for that amount."

His clients were not happy. In fact, they were livid.

"You had no right to do that! We came here to mediate. Perhaps we could have paid less! Or maybe we would have been willing to pay more. We never heard what the other side wanted."

Their lawyer was shocked. He thought they would be delighted with his quick-footed resolution. He expected that they could all leave, have a nice lunch, and enjoy the day.

Instead, the clients felt that they did not have the chance to be fully heard. And, they felt the result came too easily. They did not get the chance to use the process, to become educated, to have the back and forth of compromise, and to make a fully informed decision.

Contrast that situation with the scenario that often occurs at the end of a long day. Everyone is tired. They have emotionally advocated their positions, explored other perspectives, considered new information, and made and responded to offers, including perhaps both monetary and non-monetary elements as well.

They do not agree with the other side's ending position, or "bottom line." Nevertheless, they are close enough to reaching resolution that they can see the wisdom of "stopping the pain."

It is at this juncture, that splitting the difference represents a sound business decision. It recognizes they the parties disagree about the right amount to settle the conflict, but they are prudent business-people who wish to move on. It symbolizes the desire to achieve peace.

11. Offering Something—*Anything:* Strong Desire to Resolve

In life, when someone does something nice for us, it moves us to want to reciprocate. If your lover brings you flowers, you say "thank you" and offer a kiss, or do something kind in return. On holidays, we "exchange" gifts.

There are several books in bookstores today about improving relationships by doing something to meet one partner's needs, which will as if by magic generate the response of encouraging that partner to do something nice in return.

Similarly, the nature of negotiation in mediation is that it is typically reciprocal in nature. When one party makes an offer, the other is likely to respond in kind.

Even if moves seem to be small, the goal is to keep negotiations moving, so that progress is continually being made. You can always change your type of offer—what you do will be considered and will influence how the other responds. Sometimes, it's less about the amount than it is about the fact that you are indicating a willingness to keep going. That may be all that's needed to break impasse and reach Mediation Success.

Closing Thoughts

1. Be mindful of the drama of dollars. People want to negotiate a resolution that grants them dignity, so they can begin to heal.
2. Persons in business or workplace conflict, and in court cases, have real financial needs, concerns and fears about their future.
3. Offering to allocate dollars to meet both real economic needs and to symbolically meet emotional needs is a useful way to break down existing psychological barriers.
4. Remember the reciprocal nature of negotiation. Consider all the ways that you can creatively work towards resolution. When rational reasons seem to have been utilized to the end, the symbolism of simply moving at all might just do the trick.

CHAPTER 10

Get it Working:
Workplace Solutions

In dealing with serious conflict in the workplace, there are six core concerns that frequently emerge. These concerns run deep. They engender tension, anxiety, depression, and anger, thoughts of quitting, or even potential lawsuits.

The six most common complaints are these:

1. "I've lost trust."
2. "I don't feel respected."
3. "I am not being treated fairly."
4. "There is no communication."
5. "I have no psychic income – I don't feel valued."
6. "They never even acknowledged what they did."

These issues serve as a flashpoint to the conflict, so that resolution depends on addressing these concerns, in addition to, or in lieu of, getting the money right.

The following examples help illustrate these core concerns and suggest ways to address them to prevent conflict from escalating.

Mediation Success Rule #12:
A genuine apology will go a long way to bridge a gap caused by serious conflict.

1. Respect

When it comes to business partnerships or friction between high-level executives, one of the most frequent complaints is lack of respect. Each feels that he or she is a critical and valuable part of the organization.

When a person feels they are disrespected, treated in an undignified way, or humiliated, they become so angry they want to quit, or lash back with complaints or lawsuits.

When there is a feeling of lack of respect, there is a resulting negative impact. First, resentment builds. If it is not expressed and dealt with, withdrawal can occur—from a work group, and even from the business.

Second, resentment may be repeatedly expressed to co-workers and top-level executives, who begin to voice displeasure that key business partners are not working well together. They see the tension affect not only the relationship but also the productivity of the company.

Third, defamation lawsuits can be brought if a person is deeply concerned about harm to his or her reputation. In such cases, it's hard to put a dollar figure on the harm.

This discussion in a mediation session with three partners, Carl, Sam, and Denise, illustrates the strong reactions that a feeling of disrespect can cause.

Carl: "On more than one occasion, Denise had gotten emotional and literally walked out of our meeting! This feels totally disrespectful of our time and of the business of the partnership."

Sam: "We can't work in that environment."

Denise: "It's true, I did get emotional, and I will continue to do so. You seem to have no respect for my contribution, for the ten years of knowledge and contacts I bring to the table. You are only focused on yourselves."

I believed that Carl and Sam had a great deal of respect for Denise's experience and her network, as that was the reason they had formed the partnership with Denise. I asked them the question directly: "Carl, Sam, would you be willing to respond to Denise's concern?"

Carl: "Of course, we appreciate and respect her experience and contribution. That is why we're here."

Sam: "I can't believe Denise would even question that. She is extremely valuable to our partnership."

Carl and Sam's statements provided needed reassurance and eased the tension a bit.

Remember the principle of reciprocity in communication. When one person moves, by making a conciliatory statement, the other generally will, too.

I asked Denise if she had intended to be disrespectful to Carl and Sam. "No. I was just upset," she said. "I didn't feel like staying would be productive."

I asked: "Are you open to the likelihood that leaving a meeting, and not returning, creates bad feelings that may be hard to overcome?" Denise replied: "Well, yes, I get that."

I then asked her: "Would you be willing to commit to staying in meetings? And, if you get upset, perhaps ask for a break, and step outside, take some breaths and some time to collect yourself and gather your thoughts." She said she could do that.

Carl said: "Thank you. That is an important first step."

In the above situation, the core issue was a feeling of disrespect. One felt disrespected for her contribution, and others felt disrespect for the time they took out of their schedule for the meeting. Yet, they had never communicated the essence of what they were feeling.

When executives or teams hold meetings, it is not unusual for feelings of disrespect to arise. The key question is this: What are the actions that are causing that feeling?

Once the concerns are expressed, and each understands what actions are causing the other to feel disrespected, commitments to act differently can be put in place to prevent similar situations from occurring in the future.

How to Create an Atmosphere of Respect

The comedian Rodney Dangerfield had a famous line: "I get no respect!" It is difficult to command respect. The good news is that there are several actions you can take to create a more respectful atmosphere.

1. **Schedule meetings at a particular day and time.** Have a neutral person responsible for creating the initial agenda, with equal opportunity to add items. Consider rotating the leadership of the meeting.
2. **Obtain commitment to begin and end on time.** Agree to put away all cell phones and electronic devices, other than one person who may be taking notes about the meeting on a computer.
3. **Establish ground rules for communication.** For example, obtain agreement that when one person is speaking, others will wait for that person to finish before commenting or asking questions. Also, agree that everyone will stay the full length of the meeting. Agree on any confidentiality requirements.
4. **Bring in a communication skills trainer.** The trainer can educate everyone involved so as to increase their understanding of what kind of communication is effective vs. destructive or inflammatory. Language is key, and the who, what, when, and where of communication can make or break a good working relationship.
5. **Remember to apologize if offense has been taken.** A genuine "I'm sorry" goes a long way to smoothing ruffled feathers, and is the first step in preventing conflict from escalating.
6. **Seek a commitment from the group that if they feel disrespected, they will let the other person know and meet with them in a day or so to discuss the issue.** It may be that he or she was not aware that an action on their part left that impression. Offer information as to what occurred, how you felt, and why. Explanation, acknowledgement, and apology, if appropriate, may quickly heal the situation.
7. **Express thanks and appreciation, whenever you can.** Expressly acknowledge the value that each person brings to the team or the organization.

2. Trust

One of the most common complaints I hear is that "I've lost trust." A feeling of breach of trust leads to a sense of betrayal, and we act accordingly. Listen to what one salesperson said, who filed a lawsuit against his company:

"I did not think she was paying me what she was supposed to. I asked repeatedly, but she refused to turn over her expense records. She promised she would and then did not. She said she'd give us part, and did not. She came up with every excuse in the book. Her refusal to give me the records gave me no choice but to get counsel and file a lawsuit. I do not trust that she has been honest with me—about that, or for that matter, about anything."

In another case, one partner said, "He lied to me once. Why should I trust him again?"

Why is trust so important? We want to control our world, but we cannot. So we place our faith and our trust in certain others to act, if not always in our best interest, at least to deal with us honestly.

Is there anything wrong with walking away from someone, in business or in life, when he or she has let you down, leading you to believe you cannot trust them?

This may shock you. People are not always honest. But, I am a huge believer in what Jim Melamed, a well-known mediator, once said: "People are always motivated by positive intent. That positive intent may not have been towards YOU. Actions and behaviors are most often geared not to harm another, but rather to help oneself."

Harm to another may have been the outcome of an untruthful statement, but it was not the intent.

An employer may have the luxury of a one-time "you lie, you die" policy, but not all business and personal relationships can afford that luxury.

What am I talking about? Think about your kids. Have they ever lied to you? As a parent, have you ever experienced the following scenario?

Daughter, in tears, rubbing her arm: "Mom, Steven hit me!!"

Steven: "I did not!"

Mom: "Did you hit your sister?"

Son: "No! She's lying!!"

Daughter: "I am not! He hurt me really bad!"

One of your children was not being truthful. Did you get angry? Most likely. Did you try to seek the truth, counsel them, calm them down, and move on? Did you give them a consequence, then forgive? Did you continue to love them? I'm guessing you did.

Now let's make it a bit more challenging. Take it up a notch. Teenagers. Need I say more?

We once discovered, after receiving a call from the police at 2:00 a.m., that our teenage daughter had snuck out of the house. We had thought, strangely enough, that she was home, in bed, asleep. Another time, we found out one of our teenagers had managed to consume too much alcohol and had done some things she knew she should not have done. And yet another time, our son took the car, without telling us, and went somewhere he knew he was not allowed to go.

No surprises here, to anyone who has ever had, or been a teenager. Didn't you lie to your parents? At least once? Did they still love you, even though, really, you *knew* better? You only wanted to have some fun, to be included, to experience excitement; you certainly weren't intending to hurt your parents.

Amazingly, we all survive and still love our kids. It doesn't mean it's not hard, it's not a roller coaster ride, or that you will soon forget. It's challenging and it can be a struggle. But you *know* it's worth it. So you work at it.

Here's the secret. When you have a real, strong reason, you will work to get past mistrust. That reason is the desire to preserve a relationship, which is important to you. In the workplace, that relationship is with your business partner, your boss, or a valued employee. Preserving that relationship can also be really important to others—your clients, customers, co-workers, board members, or fellow executives.

When your continued success in business will be extremely harmed by a break in the relationship, there is a strong reason to work at repairing trust.

The Reason to Work at Repairing Trust is the Relationship

Once you have realized there is a good reason to try to get past broken trust, how can you help others to do so? Following these steps will set the right path.

1. **Ask the person to explain why he feels trust has been broken.** It is important that full expression of inner thoughts occur, so that the other will be fully aware of what he or she has done to cause the feeling of mistrust.

2. **Ask the other to tell why he acted as he did.** Perhaps there were some facts or occurrences the other person was not aware of that motivated the action. Look for the positive intent. Remember, new information can help someone to see things in a different light.

3. **Confirm the goal of each person as a good working relationship.** This long-term goal is often forgotten in the heat of anger and frustration,

when the short-term goal might be to cause the other to want to punish the other, or cause them to feel equal suffering.

4. **Encourage each to accept that things will not ever be the same.** Even though harm has been done, communication can be improved, and actions taken to start the healing process and get to a better place.

5. **Ask for a heartfelt apology.** The other person might not be ready to accept it, or to offer a reciprocal apology if warranted, but ask them to take some time to think about it.

6. **Request suggestions from each person as to what steps or conditions could be put in place to help restore trust.** Brainstorming ideas and turning them into requests that can be honored in the performance lets the people involved express their desires in a safe environment.

7. **Meet again.** Set a time to check in, to support continued openness and accountability.

Trust can be repaired, over time. Repairing trust takes communication, and action steps to provide tangible reassurance that each is committed to strong working relationship.

3. Fairness

A belief of unfairness underlies many workplace conflicts. You were not promoted when you believe you had better qualifications than one who was; you had equal qualifications but more seniority; your co-worker is unfairly "favored" by the boss and seems to receive greater benefits, plum assignments, approval for travel to seminars.

Unfair and Illegal

The notion of unfairness underlies Title VII of the Civil Rights Act of 1963 as amended. That law prohibits discrimination in employment, in hiring decisions, and in all other employment decisions.

Discrimination is illegal if it is based on certain immutable characteristics, such as age, gender, race, disability, and ethnic origin, or on one's exercise of certain "inalienable rights," such as exercise of religious beliefs. Related laws expand protection of the law to those who complain about potential discrimination. These "anti-retaliation" laws protect those who file formal complaints, or who raise informal verbal complaints, even if the underlying facts do not rise to the level of any illegal action.

Laws protect against both intentionally unfair treatment, and unintentional discrimination where there is a disparate impact—in other words, an uneven or unfair impact.

In the above circumstances, the law defines what is illegal and therefore, by definition, unfair.

Unfair But Not Illegal

What if actions clearly don't fit within something that could be called illegal? For example, consider the following scenario: there are two managers, both over 40 years of age, both male, both of the same religion and race, both without any disabilities, real or perceived. One manager is closer with the boss, because he golfs with him whenever he gets the chance. The other manager does not play golf. The "golf buddy" gets a promotion. This is not illegal, because not being a golfer is not a protected status under discrimination laws. But, it sure doesn't feel *fair*.

Sometimes, employees have a difficult time distinguishing between, or accepting, what their employer has a right to do, and what seems to them to be patently unfair.

Here is another example of a situation I mediated. The manager worked for a car dealer. An irate customer complained to his boss about the way his car purchase was handled. The boss had several past complaints about the manager, and chose to terminate him—without getting his side of the story.

It turned out that the customer had the wrong manager—the manager who got fired wasn't even present at the time of the transaction. It was handled by someone else. By the time the manager was able to convey this to his boss, it was a week or so after the termination. The boss decided to stay with his decision to terminate, anyway, in spite of the mistaken identity. He just thought it was time to part ways.

The manager filed an EEOC charge alleging discrimination based on age.

At the mediation, both parties agreed that the decision had nothing to do with age. The manager was upset that his side of the story was not obtained (he had not been heard—sound familiar?) and that he was terminated based on a mistake. But, this was in an "at-will" state, which meant as long as the employer did not have an illegal reason for the employment decision, there was nothing illegal about the action. Under the circumstances, from a legal perspective, his boss did not have to ask his side, nor did he have an obligation to re-hire him once he learned of the mistake.

The president of the company did acknowledge that he could see how it seemed unfair, and agreed that, if the situation was reversed, he would not have wanted that to happen to him. We were able to work out a financial resolution, to account for a significant amount of time the employee was unemployed after his termination. And, most significant to the employee, the employer apologized.

There are four main reasons that cause people to feel they are not being treated fairly.

1. When they are not treated equally.
2. When they are not given a chance to be heard.
3. When they are not given an opportunity to improve.
4. When policies aren't followed.

In the government setting, "due process" for non-classified employees means that the government is required to follow progressive discipline, and to provide notice of performance issues and an opportunity to be heard. That right does not exist in the private sector. Yet, if a case gets past certain legal hurdles and makes it to court, many people who sit on juries often say that they ruled in an employee's favor because "it wasn't fair what the employer did."

The statement, "Life is not fair," never sits real well to a distressed employee. If an employee can prove in court he or she was treated unfairly and illegally, certain remedies involving back pay, front pay, and compensatory damages are provided by law. For an employer, though, it can still be costly to defend a lawsuit to establish that conduct was not illegal, only unfair.

The good news is that steps can be put in place to help assure that fair decisions are made in the future.

How to Provide for Fairness—Legally Required or Not

1. **Make decisions based on objective business factors.** Consider your provable reasons, such as experience, education, performance reviews, length of service, or performance results.
2. **Explain the reasons for a decision.** Everyone has a desire to know the reasons they are being subjected to an adverse employment decision. If they do not know, they will assume the worst and likely file claims.
3. **If a decision is based on a subjective standard, recognize it.** Subjective usually doesn't necessarily mean illegal. Acknowledge that it may be perceived as unfair, but it is within your right to do so.
4. **Express continued appreciation and value.** Explain why the employee who did not get the position, promotion, etc., is still highly valued, and express the hope that they will choose to stay. Reassure the employee that he or she will have future opportunities for growth at the company. Discuss future goals.
5. **Ask if there is anything they would like to express.** It is important that the employee be allowed to express why he or she feels the decision was unfair. Hear their side. You never know, there may be new information that is learned that can influence actions going forward.
6. **Thoroughly investigate complaints.** When a complaint is made about an employee, document it and ask the employee for their explanation of what happened. Investigate thoroughly. Talk to all witnesses who may have knowledge about an event, and review relevant documents. Document the investigation and your conclusions.
7. **Communicate performance concerns—in writing.** Explain the concern, and give clear dates for expectations of improvement. Explain what the consequences will be if no improvement is made. Written documentation that is signed by the employee removes the risk that the employee thinks the concern is informal and insignificant.
8. **Consider severance.** If an employee, especially a long-term employee, has had recent performance issues so severe as to justify termination, consider offering a severance reflective of the employee's past years of service—even if your company does not have a history or policy of doing so.

9. **Mediate.** If a formal claim is asserted, offer to bring in a mediator to ensure both sides are heard, and to facilitate resolution.
10. **Establish an internal dispute resolution process.** Putting a program in place that includes mediation is the most strategic way to ensure people feel heard and have a mechanism to seek a fair resolution.

4. Communication

Communication problems abound in the workplace. There are all types of communication miscues, but the most common I hear relate to four concerns:

1. Too little communication, so that a personal connection is missing, or expectations are not understood.
2. Exclusion from communication, leading to feelings of rejection and isolation.
3. Overly public communication, causing embarrassment and anger.
4. Friction resulting from different communication styles.

Too Little Communication – Lack of Connection

On many occasions, I have been asked to work with employees to find out what the root cause of tension might be. You might be surprised how often I learn that the conflict began with frustration over a person's feeling that another employee will not reach out and make any sort of interpersonal connection.

Remember the story in the first chapter about David and George, the Executive Vice President who was too busy to spend any time talking to the manager, who had been with the organization for years and wanted a rapport with his new leader? And the story about Sam, who came in every day without so much as a "hello" or "goodbye" to his co-workers?

In each case, the other employees felt rejected and came to resent the non-communicative worker.

In a third situation of conflict I dealt with, problems began in the work relationship when a new manager arrived. It was important to her to build relationships with her staff. She tried to reach out to her employees, and establish a connection by informally stopping by their offices, and sharing some personal stories about herself and her family. Most employees responded and reciprocated.

One employee, though, had no similar stories to share. He was a very private, reserved person. He considered his manager's attempts to establish some sort of personal connection unnecessary. As a result, he was short with his new boss, who in turn felt he did not respect her. She told him she believed that he was insubordinate.

The employee complained to Human Resources that his manager was seeking to invade his privacy and was unprofessional. Ultimately, in a facilitated conversation, the employee explained that he had a few colleagues that he considered friends at work, but he had worked at the company for many years and the friendships built up over time. He stated that it wasn't that he did not like or respect his new boss, but that it was that he preferred to establish solely a professional relationship, and let the other develop over time.

Each came to a new understanding of the different needs the other had for a personal connection at work. The manager was able to take the employee's distance less as a personal rejection. The employee acknowledged that a little bit of friendliness, short of revealing personal information, would help improve their working relationship.

Each committed to be more sensitive to each other's desires.

All of the above three scenarios involved frustration with another's reluctance or refusal to have informal, casual conversations which are the normal "getting to know you" that occurs in most workplaces.

Sometimes, lack of connection can have cultural roots. In one case I handled, a Muslim doctor was at odds with the nurses on his surgical team. They claimed he was aloof, arrogant, and demeaning to them. After investigating the situation, I discovered that his cultural and religious beliefs prohibited him from touching or looking another woman in the eye who was not his wife.

What the nurses had interpreted as being aloof had a neutral explanation. Understanding the causes of his behavior allowed the parties to build a better connection and to develop ways of working together within the confines of his beliefs.

The truth is that most of us want to feel a rapport with those we work with. Some feel the need more than others. The trick is to be sensitive to that need, and when tensions arise, offer help in re-establishing boundaries and connections.

Too Little Communication – Lack of Information

When employees are not aware of information they need to know to do their jobs well, this becomes a source of frustration. "I had no idea that was what was expected of me. She never told me it was a big part of my job!" "They never told me the reason I did not get the promotion!"

When a person is not informed of reasons, it is easy to believe that it is unfair and that there is some ulterior, nefarious motive. This is the core problem that leads to resentment, withdrawal, confrontation, or complaints.

It's also not unusual for a supervisor to feel like he did communicate a performance concern or expectation, but it was done verbally and the employee did not understand how serious the conversation was intended to be.

In the workplace, more communication is better than less. Expectations are best communicated both in person and in writing.

Exclusion from Communication

Another common communication issue relates to excluding someone from communication: "They held a huge meeting on this matter and I wasn't invited!"

In one recent workplace, after discussing work issues, one employee blurted out: "They held a huge retirement party for Jim. I knew him for ten years, yet I wasn't invited!" The hurt feelings ran deep. And in another situation, the employee complained that a women's networking group had been formed in the company, but she was not on the email "d-list." This upset her greatly and she felt it was done in retaliation for a complaint she had raised in the past.

Feeling excluded leads to feelings of isolation and concern about job security. One who is excluded might wonder, "Why wasn't I asked? Are they trying to tell me something? Should I be concerned?"

More than one instance of this can lead to complaints of discrimination. Better to overinclude than to exclude. If exclusion was unintentional, explain this and correct it as soon as possible. If it was intentional, then explain the circumstances in a private meeting.

Overly Public Inflammatory Communication

How information is communicated can certainly be the root cause of tensions in the workplace. When an employee or manager yells or uses profanity, the recipients feel uncomfortable and demeaned. "She yelled at me!" "I am in a hostile work environment."

Even though the situation may not rise to the level of an illegal environment under the law, it's enough to bring employees to Human Resources with a complaint, requiring investigation and responsive action. It creates an unproductive workplace.

Where information is communicated can also be problematic. With one group conflict, an employee said, "She dressed me down right in front of the whole group! It was humiliating!" She, too, went to Human Resources with a complaint.

Finally, whom information is communicated to can be a source of friction. E-mail is a quick and efficient method of communicating, but what gets said is often less important than who is copied.

In one workplace, huge conflict developed with a group of physicians, due to the fact that one physician criticized another in an e-mail copied to the entire group. The concerns may have been valid, but the other felt that they would have been better addressed in a one-on-one conversation or in an e-mail sent to him individually. Rebuttals began, everyone was copied, and some felt they had to choose sides. Some e-mails were sent in capital letters, generally taken as an indication of yelling. Others were just uncomfortable with open airing of the conflict. Everyone complained that they were dragged into the conflict.

Communication of criticism is best done directly, and privately.

Different Styles of Communication

We are all diverse in our preferred styles of communication. In one recent conflict, the employee complained about her supervisor's informal style of communication. She wanted in-person meetings to address business needs. The employee preferred that everything be in writing, so he did not miss any important issues. In the situation of David and George, it was the other way around—the manager wanted everything done via e-mail and memos, whereas the employee wanted more informal communication.

Some of us are assertive, others passive. Some are extroverted, while others are introverted. Some are more formal than others. We all know people who are dramatic in their presentation style, and others who are reserved.

Whatever the differences, it is important that they be recognized as just that: differences in communication style, as opposed to personal animosity.

It is also helpful to realize that people react to communications in different ways. Some may need time to analyze and evaluate a message before responding. Others may become combative or take the offensive on other issues to deflect criticism. Still others may become emotional or depressed.

We all communicate differently. Understanding each person's styles can help the speaker or writer tailor their method of communication, so as to reduce friction.

Steps to Improve Communication

1. **Take time to establish a connection.** Say hello and goodbye. Have an occasional lunch with colleagues or staff. Rapport is important.
2. **Clarify expectations.** Do this both in person and in writing.
3. **Check distribution lists for inclusivity.** Include important personnel on e-mails and on invitations.
4. **Meet privately.** Express anger or frustration directly and privately before going to others.
5. **Practice e-mail etiquette.** Avoid making accusations in e-mails, and copying others who do not need to be involved.
6. **Check assumptions.** Ask the question, and seek a response confirming your beliefs before acting on them.
7. **Turn complaints into requests.** This eliminates defensive reactions, and honors the listener by allowing them to provide a considered response.
8. **Accept differences in communication style.** Whether aggressive or passive, formal or informal, help others to understand differences in style so as to tailor their method of communication, and their reactions, to be most effective.

5. Psychic Income

"I don't work here for the money. I can make this same salary any number of places. I work for the psychic income, and I'm not getting that right now."

This statement was made by Cheryl, an office manager in an insurance firm. I had been asked to mediate a conflict between Cheryl and her boss, Kathy, who owned the firm. I had not heard that phrase before and so I asked Cheryl to tell me more about it.

She said, "I am not complaining about my pay. I feel like Kathy doesn't value me. She calls me her 'right hand,' and yet doesn't include me in some of the high-level decisions and strategic planning of the company. I am told what to do, rather than invited to provide input. If I am so valuable, then *show* me!"

She thought about it a bit more, and said, "I want to feel good when I leave work each day. I want to know my boss has faith in my abilities, values, and respects me. That is what I mean by psychic income. It makes me feel good, and it's invaluable to me."

We spend so much time at work, at the office, doing what we do. The reality is that it takes more than money for us to really enjoy our careers.

Malcolm Gladwell recognized a similar need for more than money in his best-selling book, *Outliers*:

"Autonomy, complexity, and a connection between effort and reward are the three things that most people agree work has to have if it is to be satisfying. It is not how much money we make that ultimately makes us happy between nine and five. It's whether our work fulfills us… Work that fulfills these three criteria is meaningful."

Gladwell recognized that, to feel fulfilled, we need to feel good about work when we leave it each day. We need that psychic income.

So what steps can you take to build Psychic Income?

1. **Acknowledgement of value.** In mediation, Kathy expressed that Cheryl was incredibly important to her success, and the success of the firm. Kathy learned how important it was that Cheryl feel valued, and so she committed to action steps to demonstrate that. We focused on non-monetary aspects of the work relationship that could help Cheryl feel more valued. For example, Cheryl was invited to the strategic planning retreat. Her title was changed to Executive Assistant, and she was given additional responsibilities. A memo was sent out to all employees explaining Cheryl's expanded role. And, Kathy publicly acknowledged Cheryl's

contributions in a meeting with all employees. Months later, they both reported significant improvement in their working relationship.

2. **Expressions of gratitude.** "Thank you so much for all you did today. We couldn't have done it without you."

3. **Private recognition of effort.** "I appreciate all the time and effort you spent getting this project done." Recognition of effort goes a long way toward making someone feel appreciated. An unexpected bonus can have the same effect. It's not the amount, it's the thought.

4. **Public acknowledgement of value.** "Hey all—just wanted to share with you that Kelley went above and beyond to help us land this new client, and it is because of her efforts we got this wonderful new business!"

5. **Good benefits.** Good benefits provide psychic income, too. Many talented people often choose to take a government position, rather than one in the private sector, or a higher paying job, because an employer provides good medical insurance and other benefits. Government positions also provide a more stable employment environment, as employees often cannot be fired without good cause and without "due process." The stability and added feeling of security provides the psychic income of greater peace of mind.

6. **A better work schedule.** A schedule change so that a person has more flexibility, or no longer has to work nights and weekends can contribute to more quality time at home, which can lead to a greater quality of life. Consider offering a day of telecommuting per week. Added life balance provides psychic income.

I remember when I discovered I was pregnant with twins. I already had a one-year old son. I was a partner in a law firm. I was beside myself with angst, wondering how on earth I was going to handle the full-time responsibilities of being a partner and a mother of three children under two. One day, I received a phone call from an attorney who was working for a local municipality. She had received permission for her position to be converted to a "job-share" role, where each attorney would work 20-25 hours per week, and was seeking people who might be interested in interviewing for such a position.

There was only one catch: the salary was 75% less than what I was making as a partner in private practice. Yet, I jumped at the opportunity. I wanted to stay in the profession, but I was more focused on balance: the need to balance my personal and professional life was paramount. I interviewed and felt like I had been given a gift when I was offered the job. I loved the position. The "psychic income," to me, was worth more than the money.

7. **Opportunities for growth and training.** I often see charges of discrimination and retaliation, where the employee is still employed and has no actual loss in pay. Their main concern is that they were passed over for promotion, which of course would mean real income. In one recent discrimination case, the employee complained that she was denied "training opportunities." She wanted to cross-train so that she could ultimately grow in her career.

8. **Challenging work.** In another matter I handled, an employee had filed a discrimination claim a year or so earlier. After she filed the claim, her company stopped giving her projects to work on. She sat in her cubicle day after day, feeling humiliated due to the fact that she had literally nothing to do. This went on for nine months. The company maintained her same salary and benefits, but she sued for retaliation, claiming that her superiors were subtly trying to punish her for having filed a claim of discrimination against them, hoping that she would quit.

The psychological impact of being minimized for such a long period of time led her to seek counseling, take anti-depressants, and withdraw from friends and colleagues. She had real income, but felt de-valued. The complete lack of "psychic income" killed her spirit. She prevailed in her case.

Find out what brings psychic income for your employees. The great thing about psychic income is that it is not about the money—so there is no, or low, cost to meet that need.

6. Acknowledgement of Error

Over and over, I hear, "He didn't even apologize! If he had, I never would have gotten a lawyer. It wouldn't have reached this point." This is especially true where a person has experienced significant emotional distress.

At times, of course, an apology may be too little, too late. Yet, more often than not, the expression of heartfelt apology opens the door to the possibility of forgiveness—and, ultimately, the healing that comes as a result.

Think about what happens when someone apologizes. It usually looks like this:

"I'm sorry. It was not my intent to make you feel so excluded."

"Thank you. I appreciate that."

The fact is, almost always, an apology is met with either a "thank you" or a reciprocal reaction: "I'm sorry, too."

It is true that in the case of a legal claim, the wrongdoer may fear that an apology will equate to an admission of liability. One of the great gifts of mediation is its confidential nature, so a mediation setting is the perfect place for apologies to occur.

In one conflict I recently handled, an employee was let go because the company was consolidating business units. The company altered the employee's job position so as to require different skills that the employee did not possess. She filed a claim of discrimination based on her gender. Her termination paperwork said she was let go for "lack of productivity." The employee felt that was simply not true. The attorney for the company had tried to negotiate a resolution with the employee directly, but was not successful, so they came to mediation.

After the employee spoke in joint session, we took a break. Counsel for the company told me privately that the company had only put down that reason because the supervisor had to check off a box and the list of reasons didn't have category that would apply. He asked me, "Do you have any thoughts on what I should say?" I responded, "I would suggest starting off acknowledging the error, and apologizing. I think that might go a long way."

The attorney began by explaining what occurred. He said, "That was wrong. It was a mistake. You were in fact very productive. I can understand why you would be so upset. On behalf of the company, I am truly sorry this occurred. We will fix that as part of our resolution."

Tears of gratitude welled up in the employee's eyes, and she said, "Thank you. Thank you."

It was the perfect way to begin the conversation, and we were able to reach resolution.

The point is this: Relationships can be repaired. Follow these steps:

I.   Meet in person. Eye-contact is essential.

2. Remember and express the goal of a having a positive working relationship.
3. Acknowledge a mistake. This actually helps to build your credibility and symbolically provides the olive branch.
4. Offer that apology. A genuine apology will go along way to bridge a gap caused by serious conflict.

Closing Thoughts

1. There are six core concerns that usually underlie most workplace conflict situations: Respect, Trust, Fairness, Communication, Psychic Income, and Acknowledgement.
2. Addressing the core concerns helps to resolve conflict before it escalates and can improve the workplace environment, without added financial expense.
3. Investing the time to put steps in place to increase understanding and change behavior can directly improve the bottom line through increased productivity and harmony.
4. The return on investment is this: reduced turnover, legal claims, no defense costs.

PART FIVE:

Keeping the Peace

CHAPTER 11

Get to the Future: Trends in Mediation

Mediation has blossomed and has now come into its own as a form of dispute resolution in recent years.

It seems that in most every court case today, parties and their lawyers are now voluntarily electing to mediate to see if resolution is possible before pouring all their resources into taking a case to trial. Many courts even mandate the use of "ADR" (Alternative Dispute Resolution) before they will give the parties a trial date. Typically, the form of ADR most frequently selected is mediation.

Companies and organizations today are now beginning to realize the wisdom of engaging in formal mediation early on, when a claim is first brought. They understand that the earlier they engage in mediation, the greater amount of cost-savings they will realize. The emotional investment made by those involved in conflict often grows deeper over time, so the earlier each person can become fully informed, the greater the chance that the creative "Can Live With-Can Live With" resolution can be achieved that address both the financial and non-monetary issues and interests.

What Companies Can Do: Mediation Training for Managers and Human Resource Professionals

Conflict management skills are now recognized as a core competency for human resource professionals. Today, organizations are embracing the need for managers to have these skills as well. Strong conflict resolution skills de-escalate conflict and restore morale. When human resource professionals and other leaders adopt the "get it out, get it over, and get back to business" philosophy, all three aspects of conflict are addressed: the substance, the process, and the emotional psychology of conflict.

Companies can train key personnel in conflict management skills, so they can be better able to mediate internal workplace conflict at the lowest level. Skilled conflict managers face conflict when it happens, and work through it at the time, bringing a return to productivity and avoiding costly litigation.

These strong conflict management skills work well also to resolve disputes with customers, vendors, and business partners.

Organizational Mediation Policies

Both private and public sector entities are strategically choosing to include mediation as a step in their organization's internal grievance processes. Employers are now more frequently offering or even requiring mediation as a mandatory step before arbitration of disputes, or before proceeding to litigation.

For non-legal matters, where the organization has trained and skilled mediators on their payroll, there is no need to retain an outside mediator. As long as the person resolving the conflict is accepted by the parties as a neutral facilitator, and has skill and experience resolving conflicts of that kind, mediation success is possible.

For legal claims, choosing an external mediator is the commonly accepted choice. Search for a mediator with experience in resolving workplace conflict and employment disputes. As the field of mediation has become more specialized, it is not hard to find good mediators.

There are several easy-to-find resources that can provide you with individual names, rosters, or panels of mediators to help. Qualified, experienced mediators can be found through numerous organizations and websites. Through the

Internet and Google searches, consumers can locate mediators by state, by city, and by area of specialization or focus.

You can log onto mediate.com, the first and largest premier provider of mediation resources. Search "mediation providers" and find organizations with available rosters and panels of experienced mediators, along with resumes and references. You can find mediators through organizations like the American Arbitration Association, the Equal Employment Opportunity Commission, the Association for Conflict Resolution's "Advanced Practitioners" in Workplace Mediation, Mediate.com, the American College of Civil Trial Mediators, the National Academy of Distinguished Neutrals, and Institute for Conflict Prevention and Resolution (CPR.)

Some companies have policies that provide for payment of legal fees of a specified amount, generally up to $2,500 for employees to obtain legal advice if they choose when participating in mediation.

Adoption of these policies sends a strong message: We are committed to dispute resolution. We want to work things out. Please give this a try, before heading to court.

Mediation Clauses in Contracts

Mediation has been a part of residential contracts to purchase real estate in several states for many years now. Smart business lawyers are now routinely incorporating mediation clauses in the commercial contracts they draft for their business clients. Persons entering into partnerships are incorporating mediation as a dispute resolution first step.

It's Never Too Early or Too Late To Mediate

Mediation can be employed as a conflict resolution technique any time there is a serious conflict—in the workplace, in a partnership, in the conference room, or in the courtroom. Parties can voluntary agree to use the help of a mediator to resolve their disputes any time, even when they are well into a heated legal court battle. Even after judgment is rendered by a judge or jury, people can still agree to mediate to avoid the costs and uncertainty of appeal.

If you are an employee in conflict, all you have to do is ask. If you are an employer, all you have to do is offer. Where the other side offers to pay, almost always the option of mediation is accepted. You can increase the likelihood of Mediation Success by providing a ready list of mediators, or asking the other person to provide their own list or make the selection.

Remember, mediation is voluntary. Even when mediation is made mandatory by a policy or a contract requirement, all that is truly mandated is that the parties give mediation a try. Nothing will be binding on them—the outcome must be one they agree to, that they "Can Live With." All they need to do is show up. Odds are great Mediation Success will occur.

Mediation is the most effective, efficient, and respectful way to resolve disputes. Reach out and make the offer. Implement that policy. Put that clause in the contract.

Get it out, get it over, and get back to business!

CHAPTER 12

Get it Again: The Rules of Mediation Success

Okay, so you've read the book. You might be thinking, "Wow, great information, but how on earth am I going to remember this? I would definitely like to remember the information in here so I can be better at resolving all the conflicts I deal with."

Here, in a few pages, is a useful summary guide of the main points we've covered in this book.

Part One: War and Peace
No One Wins a War at Work

Conflict is adversarial and takes a huge toll. Mediation supports you in reaching an agreement that puts the matter behind you, so you can get it out, get it over, and get back to business.

I. For legal disputes, make sure everyone is aware of the significant limitations of the legal system.

2. Litigation is costly and destructive, justice is not guaranteed, the outcome is unpredictable, and it can take years to get to trial. A huge victory only ensures an appeal. Winning costs money too.
3. The court process doesn't apply to interpersonal conflict.
4. Expecting to win can lead to frustration and disappointment.
5. Principle has an inverse relationship to principal. The more resources you invest in principle, the fewer resources you have to put towards solutions and/or your business.
6. The Can Live With-Can Live With Outcome is realistic and brings peace.

Get to Peace: Mediation Success

1. Conflict results from the perception that someone is standing in the way of our success.
2. Conflict generally leads to a fight or flight reaction.
3. We tend to act in ways that create obstacles to resolution. We take an adversarial position and stick to it. We want to get to a better place, but we don't know how. We have given up hope. We are deeply invested financially and/or psychologically. We no longer see opportunity. We are not objective and so our views are discounted.
4. Mediation overcomes those obstacles, enabling people to see opportunity and instill hope.
5. Mediation creates a respectful environment where people are able to hear, receive and absorb new information.
6. Mediation works because it provides the dignity needed for others to consider changing their views and altering their position, allowing them to move on personally and professionally.

Mediation Success is resolution: a settlement agreement, improved relations at work, or even deciding whether to stay or go, and feeling at peace with your decision.

Resolution brings peace. Peace restores productivity.

Get There: The Mediation Success Process

Mediation Success embraces a complete approach to conflict resolution, working with all three aspects of conflict: substance, process, and psychology.

The Mediation Success Process has four steps:

Get it Going
Get it Out
Get it Over
Resolve the Conflict

Steps 1-3 are critical to conflict resolution, because they set the stage for success, uncover underlying interests, and address deep concerns and emotions that can otherwise block resolution.

Step #1—Get It Going: Set the Stage for Success

Select your Mediator. Choose someone who is viewed as neutral, with experience and training in resolving conflict, and strong communication skills.

Hold the initial Joint Session. This is where the foundation is laid for successful resolution, by establishing rapport, welcoming and validating the existence of strong emotion, opening the mind to different perspectives, and searching for new information.

Step #2—Get It Out: Reach the Real Issue

1. Invite sharing of perspectives, so underlying concerns and interests can be revealed.
2. Ensure each person is fully heard.
3. Mine for the gold of new information.

Step #3—Get It Over: Embrace the Emotion

Accept the display of strong emotion, and allow the emotional healing to occur that comes with venting and catharsis.

Address internal conflict, so that it can be removed as a barrier to resolving the external conflict.

Step #4—Resolve the Conflict

Put solutions in place to address the core issues that arise in workplace conflict.

Use the symbolism and drama of dollars to achieve the Can Live With-Can Live With outcome.

Part Two: The Process

Get it Going: Set the Stage for Success

Use the initial joint session to set the stage for success by focusing on the "inner game" of conflict. Address the negative thoughts that are likely in everyone's mind which serve as barriers to resolution, and in doing so, shift the dynamics.

Diffuse tension and increase the odds of resolution, in twenty minutes, by following the following steps:

1. **Create Rapport.** Make and encourage extended introductions. Provide the opportunity to establish connections between the parties and each other, and yourself.
2. **Build Trust.** Establish your credibility. Describe the confidential nature of mediation. Explain the agenda, and the process as structured, yet flexible. Describe your role as facilitating communication and negotiation, providing information, generating options for resolution, and playing devil's advocate. Reassure everyone that strong emotion is normal and acceptable, unless it reaches a level that you perceive might block potential resolution, in which case you will address those concerns in order to allow each person to move on. Use selective language to build trust, with words such as: structured, flexible, normal, acceptable, perceive, might, facilitate, generate, provide, and "play the role" of devil's advocate.
3. **Request Agreement to Three Ground Rules.** The three ground rules are (1) Refer to each other on a first name basis; (2) Allow each other to say, fully and completely, whatever they have to say, without interruption; (3) Fully disclose everything they feel is important. Language is key. Use words that open the mind: perspective, story, legitimate, allow, fully, disclose, new.

4. **Revise Expectations.** Create optimism, by sharing statistical or experiential information the strong likelihood of success. Explain that the process typically leads to learning new information, which in turn opens the door and allows people to think about resolving conflict in a way they may not have been willing to do before. Create realism, by contrasting mediation to the court process and sharing your goal of the Can Live With-Can Live With outcome.

Getting Around the Obstacles: Myths of Mediation

For Mediation Success, the conflict-resolver and the people in conflict all need to be aware of the myths and misconceptions routinely held about how others negotiate, and what will occur in the future if they do not resolve the matter.

People in conflict take positions, seeking to act in what they perceive to be their own best interests, (the positive intent) based only on what they know at that moment.

What people believe to be truths about negotiation in conflict are, in reality, only myths.

Myth #1: People Mean What They Say
Reality #1: Absolute Statements are Expressions of Current Intent

Myth #2: We Can Do Better Than the Last Offer
Reality #2: The Last Offer May No Longer Be on the Table

Myth #3: They Won't Change Their Mind
Reality #3: People Change Their Minds

Myth #4: If it Can't be Resolved Today, It Never Will be Resolved
Reality #4: Resolution is Always Possible

Myth #5: A Court Will Hear the Truth and Justice Will Prevail
Reality #5: There is No Guarantee Truth Will Lead to Justice

Myth #6: The Mediator Has the Right Answer
Reality #6: The Mediator Does Not Make the Decision

Part Three: The Psychology

Get it Out: Reach the Real Issue

The desire for money or financial security is not always the strongest motivator.

The underlying desires to be heard, to regain one's dignity, to know the "truth," to hear an apology, to achieve justice or revenge, or just to be done, may be the true motivators.

People are often not fully aware of their true motivations until they start speaking. Encourage each person to share their perspective fully, and to emphasize that mediation allows for all aspects of one's views to be considered—legal, financial, emotional, practical, and so forth.

The true driving force must be addressed for resolution to occur.

Here are the most common driving forces in workplace conflict:

1. The Desire to be Heard
2. The Desire for Acknowledgement and Apology
3. The Desire for Fairness
4. The Desire to Know
5. The Desire for Dignity
6. The Desire for Justice
7. The Desire for a Realistic Result
8. The Desire to Do Better Than Expected
9. The Desire to Be Done

Key steps to helping people get it out:

1. Tell them you will be asking them to share their perspective about what brought them to you today.
2. Share your knowledge that "perspective" is made up of all sorts of things: facts, what you recall, what you believe, how you feel, what you've heard, and what your family, friends, colleagues, or lawyers have told you, and that this is all perfectly legitimate, it just makes up each person's perspective.
3. Explain that people resolve conflicts for all sorts of reasons: legal, financial, practical, business, or emotional reasons, and that all of that is okay.

4. Stress how important it is that each person fully discloses anything and everything that is important to them.
5. Invite each person to share their perspective. Allow plenty of time for each to be fully heard.
6. Be patient. Be persistent. Be focused.
7. Listen well. Paraphrase, summarize, reflect, and clarify.
8. Ask open-ended questions, such as, "What is this about for you?" "Are there any other concerns that you haven't shared?" "Is there anything else that's important to you?"
9. Ask again. Stay with it until you get to the driving force of the conflict.

Get Through It: Emotional Stages of Mediation

Understand the emotional aspects of mediation, when they tend to find expression during the process, and how these emotions can help lead to resolution.

Be mindful of the structure, so that you can assist everyone in moving through the different emotional stages of the mediation process, listed in the A-List:

1. Anxiety
2. Anger
3. Adrenaline
4. Awareness
5. Acknowledgement
6. Analysis
7. Active Participation
8. Acceptance

If temporary pessimism strikes, provide needed reassurance that progress is, in fact, being made. This reassurance instills hope and provides optimism.

Get it Over: Embrace the Emotion

The expression of strong emotion is expected, normal and actually helpful to mediation. Accept and embrace strong emotion.

Achieve mediation success by guiding the process so that emotions are not barriers, but instead are used as positive tools for resolution.

1. Address the Internal Conflict first. There are often two distinct conflicts: the internal one and the external one. Once internal conflict has been addressed and dissipated, the mind is calmed enough to be able to absorb new information and participate in the give-and-take of the negotiation and mediation process. When we no longer have to pour psychic energy into repressing our feelings, we free up our mental abilities to address and resolve the problem at hand.

2. Embrace emotion. Encourage parties, express yourself, don't suppress yourself. Open venting and catharsis, met by non-judgmental support, is essential to allow people to move on to addressing the substance of dispute.

3. De-escalate the conflict by expressly validating the fact that strong feelings are normal and acceptable.

4. Model a calm response. Behavior is reciprocal, so your steadiness will tend to bring the other's feelings to a lower, more reasonable level where critical thinking can be brought into play.

5. Know that tears are good. Seek to understand what they signify about the internal conflict: gratitude, relief, despair, depression, embarrassment, or fear.

6. Realize that anger is natural. Acknowledge the legitimacy and accept the expression of anger. Once anger has been expressed, valuable energy for problem-solving is made available. Granting permission to be angry is unexpected, and freeing, and often has the paradoxical effect of dissipating anger.

7. Be sensitive to the knowledge that touch is powerful. If appropriate, reach out and touch. Use non-verbal skills to convey a strong message of empathy or to draw attention to the need to consider a different angle.

8. Empathy is better than sympathy. Share your own stories. Remember we all want to be understood, and to know someone else has been there. We want to believe we can survive and move past the current situation to get back to the business of life.

Part Four: The Resolution

Get the Money Right: The Drama of Dollars

When searching for possible ways to resolve workplace conflict, think about the symbolism of money. Understanding the drama of dollars allows you to be open to finding creative ways to structure a solution to meet the needs of everyone involved.

Persons in business or workplace conflict, and in court cases, have real financial needs, concerns and fears about their future. Offering to allocate dollars to meet both real economic needs and to symbolically meet emotional needs is a useful way to break down existing psychological barriers.

People want to negotiate a resolution that grants them dignity, so they can begin to heal. Consider all the ways that you can creatively work towards resolution.

1. One year's salary: Acknowledgement of Value
2. Months of Pay: A Bridge to Re-employment
3. Amounts per year of Service: Acknowledgement of Past Value
4. Compensation for Medical Bills: Acknowledgement of Emotional Harm
5. Payment of Health Insurance Premiums: Security
6. Nominal Amounts or Costs of Defense: Nuisance Value
7. Payment of Debt: Freedom to Move On
8. Payment of Tuition: A Fresh Start
9. Attorney's Fees: Cause of Financial Harm
10. Splitting the Difference: A Business Decision
11. Offering Something—Anything: Strong Desire to Resolve

Remember the reciprocal nature of negotiation. When rational reasons seem to have been utilized to the end, the symbolism of simply moving at all might just do the trick.

Get It Working: Workplace Solutions
The Six Core Concerns and Practical Strategies to Meet Them
1. Respect
2. Trust
3. Fairness
4. Communication
5. Psychic Income
6. Acknowledgement of Error

How to Create an Atmosphere of Respect

1. Schedule meetings at a particular day and time.
2. Obtain commitment to begin and end on time.
3. Establish ground rules for communication.
4. Bring in a communication skills trainer.
5. Remember to apologize if offense has been taken.
6. Seek a commitment from the group that if they feel disrespected, they will let the other person know and meet with them in a day or so to discuss the issue.
7. Express thanks and appreciation, whenever you can.

How to Repair and Re-establish Trust

1. Ask the person to explain why he feels trust has been broken.
2. Ask the other to tell why the he acted as he did.
3. Confirm the goal of each person as a good working relationship.
4. Encourage each to accept that things will not ever be the same.
5. Ask for a heartfelt apology.
6. Request suggestions from each person as to what steps or conditions could be put in place to help restore trust.
7. Meet again.

How to Provide for Fairness – Legally Required or Not

There are four main reasons that cause people to feel they are not being treated fairly: when they are not treated equally, when they are not given a chance to be heard, when they are not given an opportunity to improve, and when policies aren't followed.

1. Make decisions based on objective business factors.
2. Explain the reasons for a decision.
3. If a decision is based on a subjective standard, recognize it.

4. Express continued appreciation and value.
5. Ask if there is anything they would like to express.
6. Thoroughly investigate complaints.
7. Communicate performance concerns—in writing.
8. Consider severance.
9. Mediate.
10. Establish an internal dispute resolution process.

How to Improve Communication

The four most common communication complaints are (1) too little communication, so that a personal connection is missing, or expectations are not understood; (2) exclusion from communication, leading to feelings of rejection and isolation; (3) overly public communication, causing embarrassment and anger; and (4) friction from different communication styles.

Steps to Improve Communication:

1. Take time to establish a connection. Say hello and goodbye. Have an occasional lunch with colleagues or staff.
2. Clarify expectations both in person and in writing.
3. Include important personnel on e-mails and on invitations.
4. Express anger or frustration directly and privately before going to others.
5. Practice e-mail etiquette. Avoid making accusations in e-mails, and copying others who do not need to be involved.
6. Check assumptions. Ask the question, and seek a response confirming your beliefs before acting on them.
7. Turn complaints into requests. This eliminates defensive reactions.
8. Accept differences in communication style. Whether aggressive or passive, formal or informal, help others to understand differences in style so as to tailor their method of communication, and their reactions, to be most effective.

How to Create Psychic Income

Help employees feel fulfilled when they leave work each day.

1. Acknowledge value.
2. Express gratitude.
3. Privately recognize effort.
4. Publicly acknowledge accomplishment.
5. Offer good benefits.
6. Provide a better work schedule.
7. Offer opportunities for growth and training.
8. Give challenging work.

How to Acknowledge Error

It's difficult to move on, when there has been no acknowledgement that harm was caused. Anger, resentment and frustration builds.

Relationships can be repaired.

1. Meet in person.
2. Remember and express the goal: a positive work relationship.
3. Acknowledge a mistake. It actually builds credibility.
4. Offer an apology. This will go a long way to bridge the gap that serious conflict creates. It honors the listener, and asks for forgiveness.

Remember the reciprocal nature of an apology. It encourages the other to offer one in return.

Part Five: Keeping the Peace

Trends in Mediation for Organizations

Mediation Training for Managers and Human Resource Professionals. Train key personnel in conflict management skills, so they can be better able to mediate and resolve workplace conflict at the lowest level.

Mediation Policies. Send the message that you are committed to dispute resolution.

Mediation Clauses in Contracts. Commit to mediation before disputes arise.

It's Never Too Early or Too Late to Mediate. Mediation can be used to resolve conflict any time there is a serious conflict—in the workplace, in a partnership, in the conference room, or the courtroom.

The Mediation Success Rules

1. Go for the *Can Live With* – *Can Live With* outcome.
2. Make sure everyone is aware of the limitations of litigation.
3. Focus on the positive outcomes and opportunities that can come from conflict.
4. Language is key to setting the stage for success, so use words that reduce anxiety and build trust.
5. Being fully heard is essential to any mediation.
6. Word choice matters, so choose words that help bridge differences.
7. Revise expectations. Create optimism and encourage realism.
8. Get "no" three times before accepting a statement as a true indicator of position.
9. Invite each person to share their perspective.
10. Go to the emotion, not away from it.
11. Consider the symbolism of money.
12. A genuine apology will go a long way to bridge the gap caused by serious conflict.

ACKNOWLEDGEMENTS

There are certain people without whom I would not have been able to have this wonderful career in mediation, which, after ten years, led me to write this book. Their encouragement and support has been invaluable. Carla Snyder, an early Human Resources colleague, gave me the push I needed to break out on my own for brand-identity purposes and establish an employment mediation practice called Insight Employment Mediation. Lew Hansen, my trademark and patent lawyer, helped me select my name and protect my brand. Oliver Ross, my first mediator colleague and mentor, saw something in me that made him think, "This woman has potential!" Yvonne Gloria-Johnson, former ADR coordinator with the EEOC Phoenix District Office, trusted me to mediate my first employment discrimination case, and stuck with me all these years. Kimberly Banach-Moore, formerly with the American Arbitration Association, reached out to me to serve on their panel of Arbitrators and Mediators, when there were few women serving in those roles. Joe Clees, with the law firm of Ogletree Deakins, and Mark Ogden, with the law firm of Littler Mendelson— you are amazing leaders in the world of employment lawyers and my success is due in large part to your faith in my abilities. Jeff Brodin, you were the first to reach out to me for resolution of your company's conflict resolution needs on so many levels, and I was honored to have been your resource for the better part of ten years.

My deep gratitude also goes to my book coach extraordinaire, Henry DeVries, and to Marnie Green, my Human Resource trainer, author, and friend, for your time and efforts to help me write a book that would be a guide for the corporate, as well as the legal world. Marc Lieberman, your editing skills made me look good.

The Driving Forces of Desires section in Chapter 6 was first published in the Arizona Attorney July/August 2008 monthly magazine as the cover feature, thanks to Tim Eigo's editorial skills, and was later republished in the American College of Civil Trial Mediator's Journal of Mediation (2010). The A-List of Emotions in Mediation, discussed in Chapter 7, was first published in the American Arbitration Association's Journal of Dispute Resolution (April 2006) and later republished in their 2010 Handbook on Mediation.

Last but not least, thank you to my loving husband Rick for his support, and to my three wonderful children, Aaron, Claire and Elise. As teenagers, they taught me invaluable lessons about conflict, and made my day job much easier than my night job!

ABOUT THE AUTHOR

"Amy Lieberman is a paradigm-shifter who brings a palette of color to an otherwise black and white process, and expertly gets it done."

C-Level and HR executives challenged with resolving high stakes employment conflict consider Amy Lieberman's Alternative Dispute Resolution skills their secret to success. Among the "Best Lawyers in America," this experienced and sought-after mediator, trainer, author, and speaker enlightens and brings opposing parties together to ease tensions, protect capital, and restore balance.

Since 2001, Amy's keynotes, breakout sessions, and skilled mediation sessions have influenced thousands of individuals and organizations to peacefully resolve their conflicts and enjoy the high value benefits that flow from successful closure.

Her niche expertise on employment disputes, and a rare ability to handle legal AND interpersonal disputes, sets her apart, enabling her to provide peace of mind, enhanced business relationships, and capital savings.

Resolving tensions so that parties can preserve their dignity and move on with their lives and businesses is her highest priority.

Amy resides in Scottsdale, Arizona and La Jolla, California with her husband, Rick. Visit Amy at www.insightemployment.com, or reach out to Amy at amy@insightemployment.com.

If you'd like "hands-on" learning to build your own skills at preventing and resolving conflict, visit www.mediationsuccess.com for information about bringing training to your organization. We would love to empower you to get it out, get it over and get back to business!

Made in the USA
San Bernardino, CA
25 February 2014